2005

YOUR
OWN
WORDS

YOUR OWN WORDS

BARBARA WALLRAFF

COUNTERPOINT
A Member of the Perseus Books Group
New York

Designed by Brent Wilcox

Library of Congress Cataloging-in-Publication Data
Wallraff, Barbara.
    Your own words / Barbara Wallraff.
        p.   cm.
    ISBN 1–58243–282–1
    1. English language—Usage—Reference books—Bibliography—Handbooks, manuals, etc.   2. English language—Usage—Computer network resources—Handbooks, manuals, etc.   3. English language—Reference books—Bibliography—Handbooks, manuals, etc.
4. English language—Computer network resources—Handbooks, manuals, etc.   5. Vocabulary—Reference books—Bibliography—Handbooks, manuals, etc.   6. Vocabulary—Computer network resources—Handbooks, manuals, etc.   I. Title.
    PE1460.W227   2004
    428–dc22

2003026757

04 05 06/ 10 9 8 7 6 5 4 3 2 1

DEDICATION

Where would I be without Julian?
Someplace less stimulating, less attractive,
less functional, less fun, less warm and secure.
In countless ways he continues to earn
my admiration and win my love.
This book is dedicated to my husband,
Julian H. Fisher.
Perhaps I could have written the book without him,
but I am enormously glad that I didn't have to.

CONTENTS

ACKNOWLEDGMENTS

It takes a village not only to raise a child but also to publish a book. The chieftain of this particular village is my editor, William Frucht—a wise, kindly, and inspiring leader. And the village sorceress (I mean that in the best sense!) is my agent, Kim Witherspoon, who conjured up whatever I needed.

Many others have inhabited or at least dropped by my village, and I'm deeply grateful for their counsel, help, and support. Those whom I'm proud to see around the neighborhood (or to have seen in the past, alas) include Lisa Burrell, Grenville Byford, Elaine Chubb, Robert Cserr, M.D., Deborah Fallows, Eliane Fontes, Joshua Friedman, Orit Gadiesh, Bryan A. Garner, Patricia M. Godfrey, Norm Goldstein, Benjamin Healy, Alexis Hurley, David Joel, Andrew Johnson, Michael Kelly, Samuel Jay Keyser, Rich Lane, Linda Lowenthal, Chris McMurry, Kermit Midthun, Glenn Mott, Cullen Murphy, Jeff Newman, Eleanor Gould Packard, Richard Parker, Robin Parker, Steven Pinker, Katya Rice, William A. Sabin, Jesse Sheidlower, David Shoemaker, Allan M. Siegal, Martha Spaulding, Charles F. Wallraff, Evelyn B. Wallraff, Bill Walsh, William Whitworth, Jon Zobenica, and all the people—yes, all of them—who have sent me letters and e-mail at Word Court and *Copy Editor* newsletter.

CHAPTER ONE

My Own Words

Not long ago I received this letter:

"I am appalled by the free use of the word *gentleman*. I've been hearing it used more and more, by the police and the news media, in reference to men who have broken the law. But I have never been more shocked or disgusted than the other day when I heard a local newswoman refer to the accused kidnapper-murderer of Samantha Runnion, a five-year-old child, as a *gentleman*. Has *gentleman* now replaced *man*? My dictionary defines the word as 'a man of good breeding.' Am I old-fashioned, or is my dictionary outdated?"

And here's the way I responded in my Word Court column in *The Atlantic Monthly:*

Neither. But you're right that *gentleman* turns up in many inappropriate contexts. For instance, on a *Today* show segment about the Runnion case, Katie Couric interviewed Mike Carona, the sheriff of Orange County, California, where Samantha disappeared. She asked about a suspect being sought, "Any chance he might turn himself in?" and Carona responded, "I would hope that he would. There's only two options in my book. This *gentleman* turns himself in or we're going to track him down and bring him in—bring him into custody."

The following month, on CNN, Connie Chung talked with Sheriff H. F. Cassell, of Henry County, Virginia, about the recent abduction of nine-year-old Jennifer Short and the murder of her parents. She asked about someone the sheriff's department had interrogated, "Did this *gentleman* have a key to their house, or was he able to get in easily, do you know?"

Let's remember—and be glad—that law-enforcement officers and journalists have been trained to speak of people respectfully. Let's remember, too, the presumption of innocence that is central to our legal system. Once someone is convicted of a heinous crime, words quite different from *gentleman* apply. Often, though, using *gentleman* instead of *man* is just a silly genteelism, and it's not much worse in reference to a criminal investigation than it is in this recent citation from *The Sacramento Bee:* "Not so routine is the 800-pound man the Coroner's Office received not long ago. Firefighters had to cut a hole in the *gentleman*'s trailer to get him on his way." As you suggest, *man* would have been a better word choice in all these quotations.

How do I come up with an answer like that? The reference works that are shelved and piled on all sides of my desk and electronically bookmarked in my computer tempt me to believe that what I do is pretty simple. If someone asks me about the spelling, pronunciation, or meaning of a word, I can look it up in the seven major contemporary American English dictionaries in existence. In fact, I have the dictionaries on my computer, so I don't even need to go over to the bookshelf to check them all.

If the person wants to know about the word's history, I can review the *Oxford English Dictionary*—actually, the *OED* lexicographers' latest scholarship, available online—or books about etymology or the dozen historical or out-of-date dictionaries I have squirreled away. If I need to find out where the word fits conceptually in the language, I can check a dictionary of synonyms or any of three fat thesauri, compiled according to different principles, or the three other thesauri on my computer. Or maybe what I want to learn about the word—or about a phrase, or a way of expressing something—can be found in some of the thirty or so stylebooks and usage manuals on my shelves, in one of my dictionaries of slang or idioms, or in a visual dictionary, a grammar book, a learners' dictionary (for non-native-speakers), or a writing guide.

Or maybe I can find it out from one of the ever-proliferating reference Web sites bookmarked in my computer. Or I can type the word or phrase into an online database or search engine and see how it is used in practice—in the written world at large or in edited media, as I prefer.

But how to decide what to do when? And what if I look up a word in the seven major dictionaries or half a dozen of my favorite usage manuals and they don't agree?

If I were to reply to all of my correspondents in a thorough and scholarly way, I would be explaining day in and day out that some authorities say X but others say Y, and that we each have to make up our own mind. This is not what most people want to hear. In my experience, people tend to believe there's one solution to every problem, one right answer to every question, and if I can't tell them what it is, that just goes to show how ignorant I am.

Knowing full well that respectable opinions vary and that if I wanted to I could usually give an equally convincing but different answer, I've gotten used to telling people what *I* think. Although you might imagine that this would be easier than reporting on what everybody else thinks, it is not. Language is collaborative: words mean what most of us think they mean. Communicating clearly requires that there be someone to communicate to, who understands us the way we intended to be understood.

What I think is less what *I* think, therefore, than what I gather is the consensus of informed opinion. In the case of *gentleman,* dictionaries define it the way my correspondent says, give or take; the quotations come from an online database; and standard reference works including *Garner's Modern American Usage, The New York Times Manual of Style and Usage,* and the *Associated Press Stylebook* warn against using *gentleman* instead of *man* where the intended sense is just "adult male human being." Simple.

But my supposed consensus isn't necessarily the last word. As soon as the exchange about *gentleman* was published, readers' thoughts came pouring in. One person wrote:

> "Have you and the author of the letter about *gentleman* both for-gotten about irony? While the police and the press have to uphold the presumption of innocence, they can do so in their speech by substituting polite usage for the terms more genuinely expressive of their feelings, such as *scumbag.* I am surprised that you ne-glected to consider that element."

Another brought up a related point:

"The misuse of *gentleman* gets our attention because it is relatively new, but what about the equally egregious misuse of *lady*? Terms like *cleaning lady* and *bag lady* are still common (although we are unlikely to say *lady lawyer* or *lady astronaut*). Since *lady* was originally paired with *lord*, and *gentlewoman* with *gentleman*, in olden days *cleaning lady* would have been an oxymoron. And it would seem that *ladies* and *gentlemen* are etymologically mismatched."

That seeming mismatch, in fact, came about centuries ago when *lady* began to be used in more and broader contexts while *lord* did not. All the same, in theory a lady has, or had, higher social standing than a gentleman—and that is why the set phrase is *ladies and gentlemen,* not *gentlemen and ladies,* as we might expect it to be from the similar set phrases *Sir or Madam* and *he or she.* But perhaps that's a story for another time.

Yet another person wrote:

"Reading your column about improbable *gentlemen* reminded me of a news story I once heard, in which a vicious dog had gone on a rampage and '*had to be put to sleep* with a butcher knife.'"

Worthy addenda all. I learn a lot from the people who read the column closely and let me know how it sits with them. And here's one more thought-provoking response to my response:

"How dispicable to compare a child raping kidnapping monster (innocent until proven guilty) to a person who weighs 800 pounds and lived in a trailer. (obviously already convicted of these 'crimes' by you) Except for being massively overweight and not living in a house what was your reason to conclude (or have your readers conclude) that the deceased man was not a gentleman?

"The other people listed were suspected criminals of the worst sort. How can you even suggest that it is 'not much worse' than using 'gentleman' for heinous murderers, than for the poor fellow in the Sacramento Bee that you use as a comparison. What do you think this does to his family to read something like this. what kind of creep would write this? What was the 'crime' of the dead man that made you say that he should be called a man and not a gentleman? How do you know that ? Was it just that he was fat, or because he was poor? Also I have never heard 'genteelism' used as a real word, but genteel would never be a word i would use for a woman making use of a poor, fat dead guy to make a snotty, arrogant, sports club member point.

"Please explain yourself.

[Signed,]

"Fat and poor, yet much more a gentlewoman in Vermont— even if my grammar stinks"

Ouch. (This last e-mail is reproduced here verbatim except that I have left off the correspondent's name. Nearly all the other letters in the book have been edited the same way my own writing has been; you'll be able to tell which ones have not.) I never replied directly to "Fat and poor," because I didn't know what to say. I couldn't agree more that in fundamental ways we are all created equal—but I wasn't talking about that, I was talking about English usage. And yet even I, Ms. Expert Communicator, failed to make myself clear this time, to this person, for my point about the fellow who died in his trailer was that the word *gentleman* was less respectful in context than plain, simple *man* would have been. "Fat and poor," are you there?

I've chosen *gentleman* as my point of departure because the word is so highly nuanced and because, clearly, its nuances matter to people. Depending on context, it can—as readers took pains to remind me—be serious or ironic, polite or insulting, formal or affectedly refined ("genteel"). Though the word primarily has to do with social class, it is not our own class but our facility with such nuances that shapes our response to it.

Class, or something like it, is often invoked to explain what different levels of language—different ways of phrasing the same thing—say about the people using them. I believe I've even invoked it myself. Yet this line of thought has always made me uncomfortable. What's more, saying that the "better" classes use English in particular ways—that they use good-quality standard English—and that therefore we should too is a weaker argument than standard English deserves, because Americans don't hold the well-bred in particularly high esteem. We are more likely to look up to talented musicians and athletes and actors and chefs, self-made billionaires, and people who have changed the world. We don't revere class; we admire people who make the most of their potential. That potential need not have anything to do with language—although the talented but inarticulate tend to have agents who wield language effectively on their behalf. Making the most of most kinds of potential does, however, involve communicating with subtlety.

A much stronger argument for standard American English—for understanding it, speaking it, and writing it—is that as inhabitants of a big, diverse nation, we need to share a means of communication. And here it is. Most of our literature, centuries' worth, is written in standard English. The day's news arrives in spoken or written standard English. Business memos and textbooks and cookbooks and minutes of school-board meetings and the instructions that now come with practically anything you buy are written in standard English, or at least English that is trying to pass for standard.

Talk and write however you want with your family, your friends, your co-workers. Use the slang and the jargon they use. Or adopt, slyly, the verbal tics of people for whom you and yours feel contempt. Invent private idioms: refer to strangers who look alarming as *Canadian* ("Dear, do you think the man who seems to be following us is Canadian?"), exactly because in ordinary usage that word's connotations are inoffensive. Whatever. When you're trying to communicate with or understand people you don't know well, though, your best bet is standard English. As all my mail about *gentleman* shows, even that is far from foolproof—but it's your best bet.

This idea is often expressed by language mavens, and where they tend to be going with it is that everyone should learn the linguistic niceties that they know. I mean, for instance, such niceties as how to spell *despicable*. Such niceties as that *child-raping*, when used as an adjectival compound, should be hyphenated. That a sentence beginning with *How despicable* followed by an infinitive is exclamatory, and should preferably end with an exclamation point. That the end punctuation of a sentence should come after, not before, a related parenthetical phrase. That the first eleven words of *Except for being massively overweight and not living in a house what was your reason . . .* are a dangler. ("Fat and poor," please forgive me— I don't ordinarily correct people's grammar unless they ask me to. But if you want others to perceive you as the gentlewoman you know yourself to be, you'll need to express yourself differently.)

I care about linguistic niceties, and I know more of them than most people do. Many of them, I've regretfully concluded, serve about the same purpose as a secret handshake: they identify language mavens to one another. How many and what kinds of niceties a person observes indicate degree and type of language mavenhood. That the sentence before last ended with *one another* and not *each other,* for instance, might be a hint that I hew to fairly traditional standards. That the previous paragraph contains four sentence fragments is a hint that my standards aren't as traditional as they might be.

But let's set all that aside and take the position that language exists to serve us, not the other way around. Let's say that the purpose of using good-quality standard English is to get our particular message across, to express ourselves just so, rather than to flaunt our knowledge of the nuances of language for their own sake. No two people use English alike; not even any two people who use standard English use it alike; and the differences mean something, whether the speaker knows it or not. Where do you want to be on the continuum of laid-back to scrupulously correct? Of earthy to high-minded? Of state-of-the-art to for-the-ages? Not only are our situations and moods and viewpoints constantly shifting, but so is the language that expresses each of these qualities.

Hence this is not a book about how to use the language faultlessly, precluding all objections to how you express yourself. Someone can always object. As we'll see, not even the leading authorities on language agree on many things. Some respected American reference works will tell us to use the serial comma—the comma before *and* in a series like *authorities, ignoramuses, and those in between*—and others tell us flatly not to. The respected reference works don't agree on how to spell hundreds of words, exactly what to hyphenate or capitalize, what some words mean and how to use them properly, whether certain constructions are back-slappingly informal or direct and conversational, whether others are pretentious or simply correct, and whether yet others toady to radical interest groups or show nothing more than a decent respect for egalitarianism. Widely beloved guides to writing and speaking disagree about what fundamental principles of communication we should all keep in mind.

Rather than simply choosing one expert and going along with whatever he, she, or it says—and never mind that no source has an answer to every language question that might come up—maybe you'd prefer to have informed opinions of your own. This book is about how to.

Gentleman plunged us, total immersion style, into the maelstrom of American English. But now let's climb out, dry off, and go look for some questions that have easy, definite answers. These turn out to be in shorter supply than you might think.

CHAPTER TWO

Secrets Dictionaries Know

I'm flattered when people write me for language help, but sometimes I'm puzzled, too: why didn't they just look in a dictionary or check a dictionary Web site? And then I realize that it's not necessarily obvious, even to language professionals, what to look up.

"Perhaps you can spare a minute either to backstop me or to shoot me down. As a newspaper editor, I have a continuing wrangle with a copy editor who persists in reducing *a couple of* to *a couple*— which, to me, is at best slangy. I can't convince this editor that she's putting rough edges on our prose, and my boss is taking a laissez-faire attitude on the matter. I've managed to persuade her to leave *a couple of* alone in copy that I write, but now I catch her making the *of* deletion in a column by, of all people, William Safire. What do you think?"

Try looking up *couple* in your dictionary. The question you're asking amounts to whether it's proper to use *couple* as an adjective, and of course dictionaries give part-of-speech labels.

> The adjectival usage of *couple* is informal, according to four of the seven major contemporary American dictionaries. One of the other three, *Merriam-Webster's Collegiate,* in a note arguing that the usage is not actually nonstandard, calls it "an Americanism, common in speech and in writing that is not meant to be formal or elevated." Your copy editor, it seems to me, needn't be required to *add* the word *of* to the work of, say, Dave Barry or the *Car Talk* guys, if your paper happens to run their columns too. But I, and implicitly five of the seven major dictionaries, agree with you that she should not be making a habit of lopping it out.

As this exchange suggests, a second problem with using "the dictionary" to get a definitive answer to a language question is that the major contemporary American dictionaries don't speak in unison. In alphabetical order the seven of them (and the abbreviations I use for them) are *The American Heritage Dictionary,* fourth edition (the *AHD*); *Merriam-Webster's Collegiate Dictionary,* eleventh edition (*MWC*); the *Microsoft Encarta College Dictionary* (*Enc*); *The New Oxford American Dictionary* (*NOAD*); the *Random House Webster's Unabridged Dictionary,* second edition (the *RHUD*); *Webster's New World College Dictionary,* fourth edition (*WNW*); and *Webster's Third New International Dictionary* (*W3*).

Each of these is a sizable American dictionary that has been kept current or is widely used by language professionals, or both. Obviously, there are also many smaller dictionaries, including more than a few derived from these seven, plus a wide range of specialized dictionaries. And there's the *Oxford English Dictionary,* second edition, which some people think of as the best all-around dictionary in existence. It's certainly the biggest, but I consider it specialized, because it's less authoritative on current American meanings than it is on word histories.

All seven dictionaries are available on CD-ROM, either together with the print edition or as a separate product—at least, they are available for Windows machines. (People who use the Apple Macintosh platform aren't totally out of luck, but for more about that, please see Chapter Three.) If you tend to use a dictionary while writing or reviewing word-processed documents, CD-ROMs are wonderful, because you can install their contents on your computer's hard drive and call up information about words by clicking on them in your text or typing them into a window. But it's nice to have the print edition, too, for Scrabble games, for skimming, for serendipity, and to settle arguments when the computer is turned off.

(In researching what follows, I've sometimes used the print dictionaries, sometimes the CD-ROMs, and occasionally Web sites. The editions I've used are up to date, but they're not necessarily the latest "copyright printing": some dictionaries are revised slightly every year or so. Also, when quoting from them I have spelled out most abbreviations and made formats consistent, so that this book will be easier to read. Please don't mistrust me if what I say doesn't *exactly* match what's in your copy of that dictionary.)

Twenty Questions

I had imagined we could begin exploring the American dictionaries by looking at what they have in common. To that end, I plucked from my mail twenty examples of questions that dictionaries can undoubtedly answer and that the seven might even answer the same way.

"Should the *a* in *anthrax* be capped? I think of the word as a proper noun and therefore cap it, but I'm not so sure that I'm correct in doing so. Thanks!"

Why, no, everyone lowercases it. It's not a proper noun, as you'll see if I cite the word's etymology as outlined by *The American Heritage Dictionary,* which is the dictionary I usually turn to first: "Middle English antrax, *malignant boil,* from Latin anthrax, *carbuncle,* from Greek."

❖

"Is there such a word as *off-putting*? I understand the implied definition to be 'distracting, disturbing, mildly upsetting.' I have heard this word used by well-educated people and have seen it in print. What is your judgment?"

Yes, indeed, this word is in all seven of the dictionaries, defined just about as you say.

Can it be, I wondered as I drafted that response, that this correspondent has a little paperback condensed dictionary that doesn't include *off-putting*? Anyone who doesn't use a full-size dictionary and can't find one on the Web (we'll get to that in Chapter Four) has no business being off-put by unfamiliar words.

OK, you caught me: *off-put* is not a word, at least not according to any of our dictionaries.

❖

"Is it correct to use the word *on* before a date or day of the week? For example, is it correct to say 'We will arrive *on* Tuesday'? The meaning doesn't change if you omit the word *on:* 'We will arrive Tuesday.' A grammar instructor of mine long ago told me one places items *on* a table; one does not place anything *on* a day. I am seeing and hearing *on* used this way more and more. Can't it be omitted?"

Whether *on* can be omitted from a sentence like your example is a different question from whether there's anything wrong with including it. All of the major dictionaries give a range of meanings for *on,* and each of them says something about its being used as a preposition (as you're using it) to indicate time. The *Random House Webster's Unabridged,* which gives the largest number of meanings for the word as a preposition—thirty-one, including three informal uses and one specialized nautical one—gives as the twenty-sixth meaning "(used to indicate time or occasion): *on Sunday; We demand cash on delivery.*"

"On CNN this morning a military person was commenting on U.S. soldiers' finding barrels of chemicals intended for killing 'mosquitoes and . . . *airborne vermin.*' I'm quite familiar with the former but have no idea what the latter can be. Can you help me?"

The first mental image that *airborne vermin* brought me was what you pictured too, I'll bet: rats with wings. But all seven dictionaries make clear that *vermin* can include insects. For instance, *Merriam-Webster's Collegiate* gives among its definitions "small common harmful or objectionable animals (as lice or fleas) that are difficult to control." So the only problem with the phrase you heard is that maybe *mosquitoes and . . . vermin* is redundant.

To my surprise, unanimity among the dictionaries ended with that question. Naturally, dictionaries concur about lots of things—how to spell every word in this sentence, for example. But those things aren't what people tend to wonder about. (What people do wonder about can be startling, though, can't it?) Don't worry: I'm not mounting a campaign to get you to look up all your word questions in seven dictionaries. We're just exploring what the major versions of a fundamental language-reference tool have in common and what they don't.

"I definitely do not claim to be an authority on grammar, but I can find no support for using *disrespect* as a verb. I often hear people, even folks in the media, say things such as 'He *disrespected* her.' Its use is becoming more prevalent, and I am beyond being annoyed."

Although *The New Oxford American Dictionary* labels it *"informal,"* the verb *disrespect* appears in all of our dictionaries, and none of the others so much as hints that it's anything less than standard. (I wonder if the informal or slang verb *dis* has turned you against *disrespect,* too.) *Merriam-Webster's Collegiate,* which for most words gives the date of the earliest citation it has, traces the verb *disrespect* back to 1614—seventeen years before its earliest citation for the noun. Does its antiquity change your opinion of this verb?

"I recently took part in an intense debate at the University of Iowa Writers' Workshop. Is the word *buttocks* singular or plural? Is there such a thing as a *buttock*? Please advise."

If you happened to look this up in the *RHUD,* I can understand why you might be confused. It says:

Usually, *buttocks.*
a. (in humans) either of the two fleshy protuberances forming the lower and back part of the trunk.
b. (in animals) the rump.

But although that seems to say that either of the protuberances is usually referred to as *buttocks,* the other dictionaries clearly indicate that there is such a thing as a human *buttock,* and that if you're like most of us, you have two of them.

"It seems to me that nowadays there is a plethora of the use of the word *plethora.* Instead of employing it to denote 'an excess of,' many writers seem to be using the term with the more positive meaning 'a plenitude of.' To give but one example, in Mike Wallace's book *A New Deal for New York,* the author envisages the 9/11 epicenter's renaissance with the construction of a 'magnificent new Fulton Center hub . . . into whose aerated and reorganized chambers would flow a *plethora* of north-south lines.' Present-day downtown New York may be a little too quiet for our liking, but would we really like to stuff it with a *plethora* of new transportation lines? Is my understanding of this misuse correct?"

Yes, it is. At least, all seven dictionaries use words like "excess," overabundance," and "superfluity" to define the word. *MWC,* however, says that *plethora* "also" means "profusion, abundance." In this dictionary's definitions, however, "also" specifically signals that a meaning is "closely related to but . . . less important than the preceding sense." If you and I approved of Mike Wallace's usage, we might seize on *MWC's* definition eagerly. But we'd have to ignore the balance of opinion, according to which the word remains pejorative.

"In a recent magazine article, in an otherwise literate and readable passage, I ran smack into *fulsome* used in the sense of 'generous' or 'complete.' I encounter this more and more often, and for me it sinks an otherwise good piece of writing. *Fulsome* to me denotes 'foul,' as in an overflowing sewer, so that *fulsome praise* used correctly suggests a somewhat tainted compliment. I would welcome your judgment on this."

> *Fulsome* is a booby trap, because anyone who doesn't happen to have looked it up and has never been corrected is sure to assume from the sound of the word that fulsomeness is a good thing. Whether or not you and I like it, this idea is gaining ground. *Webster's Third* gives both positive and pejorative meanings for the word without comment. The other dictionaries also give both meanings, though they include a warning that readers may misinterpret or disdain those who use it in a positive sense.

"An announcer at our local classical-music station programs his music around anniversaries of composers' births, deaths, premieres, and the like. Thus he might introduce 'Toccata and Fugue in D-minor by Johann Sebastian Bach, who was born *today* in 1685.' Bach was not born *today.* Similarly, Aaron Copland did not die *today;* we lost him in 1990. Issue your injunction and I will serve it on the perpetrator."

> I'd love to—to my mind *today in 1685* is absurd. But if you think the way that announcer does, meanings given for the adverbial use of *today* in *MWC* ("on or for this day"), *Enc* ("*on this day:* on or during this day"), and *W3* ("on or for this day: on the present day") aren't likely to show you the error of your ways.
>
> People who agree with you and me about what *today* means could easily have written those definitions, never imagining that anyone would interpret the word the way your announcer does.

You might enlist the help of the other dictionaries, though, to make your point. For instance, the *RHUD* gives the definitions "on this present day" and "at the present time." I like to think these (and also the definitions in the dictionaries not cited here) rule out the likes of *today in 1685.*

"I am writing re the annoying and ubiquitous use of the word *on* in place of other prepositions such as *for*—as in 'I am waiting *on* a bus.' I always thought that to be waited *on,* you had to be either royalty or a customer in a restaurant. As a part-time legal transcriptionist, I always change *on* to *about* or *in reference to,* etc., in such contexts as 'I have your file *on* Mr. Jones.' Lately, however, I've been feeling more and more like a lone voice. Help!"

Excuse me . . . In legal documents that you transcribe (*transcribe* being defined by the *AHD* as "to make a full written or typewritten copy of [dictated material, for example]"), you're pretending that people who said *on* instead said *in reference to*? Um, better not. All of our seven dictionaries give the *about* or *in reference to* meaning of *on* without any notes or cautions about it. On (ahem—not *in reference to,* please) this point I'm afraid you *are* a lone voice.

Wait on is a different case. Dictionaries treat it under *wait*— some in the main entry, with examples that demonstrate (or don't) the use of *wait on,* and others as a "phrasal verb" defined separately. The *AHD, MWC,* and *NOAD* either implicitly or explicitly accept as standard *wait on* in contexts like your example; *Enc* and *WNW* label it *"informal";* the *RHUD* notes that it is "sometimes considered objectionable in standard usage"; and *W3* doesn't give any clear direction one way or the other.

"*Wait on* a bus" grates on my ear too, and I wouldn't say it. But, alas, you and I have no definite basis for objecting when others use it, except in formal contexts. Maybe that means it's OK to *wait on* a bus—just not a limo?

"The corruption of *hark back* into *hearken back* (or *harken back*) in speech and print is becoming so common that when I hear or see *hark back* used correctly I feel an instinctive urge to congratulate the person for proper usage. I am surprised at how frequently this error comes from people who are otherwise literate and even erudite. Is this particular vulgarization destined to win the day? Should we give up without a struggle, or is there a chance that this juggernaut of decay can be halted?"

I'm with you in preferring *hark back,* and the *AHD, Enc,* the *RHUD,* and *W3* agree with us, giving only *hark* with *back. NOAD* allows *hearken back; MWC* gives as a meaning of *harken* "hark back," remarking that it's "usually used with *back*"; and *WNW* gives *hearken back* but notes that it's "objected to by some." So although that juggernaut has been busy, it has yet to triumph. Dictionaries don't support us unanimously, but we're not eccentric for preferring *hark back.*

"When—and why—did *Daylight Saving Time* become *Daylight Savings Time*? I grew up using the former expression. The latter sounds awkward to me."

You and me both. But first please note that the seven dictionaries agree that none of the words in the phrase should be capped. (People are tempted to cap the words because the initialism *DST* is capped, but initialisms follow different rules.) Also, the entries vary with respect to hyphenating *daylight saving*—though, as I will discuss later in this chapter, we'll have to look at the dictionaries' "front matter" to decide what the presence or absence of hyphens means in each case. Furthermore, five dictionaries give the version with *savings* in it as a lesser or an equal variant; some also give *daylight saving, daylight savings,* and *daylight time* as variants.

Does that tell you everything you need to know—or everything and more? I'd say the array of possibilities is annoying rather than liberating. But at least no one thinks *daylight saving time* is wrong.

From here on out, things get worse and worse—except "worse and worse" isn't really the right idea. Again, it's only natural to wish that all the authorities agreed on particular points about language. (In fact, it's natural to wish that all the authorities on anything agreed on everything.) They don't, though, and if we really care about understanding our language, it's essential to recognize that.

"Television ads often use the word *dairy* for dairy products, as in 'I take one little pill daily, and now I can enjoy *dairy* again!' Do people really talk like that, or just ad writers? Will we soon consume *farm* instead of farm produce or *ocean* instead of fish? A dairy is where cows live; let's leave it that way!"

In four dictionaries *dairy* is not defined as anything that can be consumed, but *Enc, NOAD,* and the *RHUD* say that the word can be used to mean "dairy products." (The *RHUD* alone specifies that the word has to do with "Jewish dietary law.") This variation suggests that *dairy* meaning "dairy products" hovers at the edge of contemporary mainstream English.

Naturally, lexicographers are constantly scouring print and other sources for new words and new uses of old words, to keep their dictionaries up to date. They don't invent words, so dictionaries follow, rather than lead, the language. But unless the lexicographers have evidence (as the *RHUD*'s seem to have here) that the word is seen primarily in specialized contexts, they won't necessarily make clear what sector of society a word has come from. You'll find "subject" or "field" labels like *"medicine"* and *"geology,"* but I doubt you'll ever find one that reads *"ad copy."*

"I was surprised to see an article in today's *New York Times* include the following: 'Does the whole enterprise give Mr. Lowry *agita*?' I heard the term *agita* quite a bit when I was growing up in an Italian family in Boston's North End, but when did this word (which means 'stomach aggravation due to stress') become part of American lingo?"

The *AHD, MWC, Enc,* and the *RHUD* have entries for *agita,* defining it much the way you do; the other dictionaries don't include it. It's another word on the edge of the mainstream.

Oddly, dictionaries absolutely must include all the words that everyone understands. Words that some people have never heard and will find perplexing are the ones most likely to be left out.

"While recently editing a document at my law firm, I became puzzled. In law, one uses the word *proceedings* to designate case-related events—for example, *court proceedings, discovery proceedings.* The question that arose was, Should *proceeding* be singular or plural?

It seems as though an event should be referred to as *a proceeding* rather than *proceedings."*

NOAD defines only *proceedings* and not *proceeding* as a noun. All of the other dictionaries give some definitions, often law-related ones, that they specify as pertaining to the plural noun, and also some for *proceeding*—but they're a long way from concurring on exactly when the plural should be used and when the singular. Because you're talking about a specialized legal context and you work in a law firm, if I were you I'd quiz a few lawyer colleagues whom I respect about what sounds right to them, and follow their advice.

"What do you think of *scared* as an adjective? I constantly hear it used in sentences like 'I'm *scared* to confront him about his drinking' and 'I'm *scared* of him.' The second example sounds extremely childish. Shouldn't we be using *frightened of* or *afraid of,* or *afraid to* with a verb?"

The *AHD* says that *scare* is "less formal" than *frighten,* and *W3* says that it is "often equivalent to *frighten* in conversational use," but none of the other dictionaries draws any distinction between the words according to the level of language each occupies.

Standard English contains a range of ways to say practically anything, and hardly ever are any two of them exactly equivalent. "I'm *scared* of him," "I'm *frightened* of him," "I'm *afraid* of him," "I'm *fearful* of him," "I'm *terrified* of him," "He *makes me nervous,*" and "I'm *timorous* in his proximity" all have their uses. The fact that most dictionaries let *scared* pass without comment, whereas they label *mommy* and *scaredy-cat,* for instance, *"informal"* or the like, tells us that *scared* is within the bounds of standard English.

In fact, according to respectable schools of thought, the simplest way of saying something is usually the best. If you out-and-out don't like the word, you're within your rights, but ... are you content to be thought of as possibly stuffy and certainly somewhat formal?

"I am concerned about the ever-increasing use of the word *about* in the sense of 'on the subject of, concerning' (definition from *Webster's New World Dictionary*). I worry that this simple word is frequently used as a substitute for rigorous expression and probably for logical thought. This letter was precipitated by a news report this week about arguments before the Supreme Court on the issue of open primaries. An attorney proclaimed, 'A primary is *about* voters and elections!' Surely the Supreme Court deserves a more compelling argument."

Four of our dictionaries either define *about* in ways that allow the uses you deplore or give examples of them: "It's all *about* having fun" (*NOAD*), "<poker is *about* money —David Mamet>" (*MWC*). Will it cheer you to know that *Enc* and *WNW* present *be what something is all about* as an *"informal"* expression?

Better still, *Enc* and also the *AHD* include usage notes warning against loose uses of *about.* The *AHD*'s concludes: "Fifty-nine percent of the Usage Panel rejected this use in the example *A designer teapot isn't about making tea; it is about letting people know that you have a hundred dollars to spend on a teapot.*" If you want to try to bring other people around to your views on *about,* that's what to tell them. And while you're at it, you might point out that *for* could replace each of the two *about*s in the *AHD*'s example sentence, with no harm done to the thought expressed or to the English language.

That such a simple substitution is possible, however, suggests that not all new uses of *about* are less "rigorous" and "logical" than more traditional wording. For my own part, I get a kick out of spouting *about* at times. I mean, how else would you say "This usage is about adding a touch of irony, not about being correct"?

"My question is about *into* and *in to*. Are they interchangeable? Or are there times when only *in to* is correct other than when the *to* is part of an infinitive?"

WNW offers a succinct explanation of the basic difference between *into* and *in:* "when the idea of motion from outside to inside is intended, *into* is generally preferred." *Enc,* though, is likely to leave you with the impression that the two words don't overlap in meaning at all. None of the other dictionaries explains how the two words differ. And none of the seven supplies an answer to your question about *into* and *in to.* Remind me and we'll look in a usage manual when we get to Chapter Six.

"In the past few years I've noticed people using the verb *wax* as a word meaning 'talk'—specifically, to blather on about something. Dictionaries I consult define *wax* as 'become' or, as in *a waxing moon,* 'grow in size or intensity.' These are the definitions I have always associated with *wax.* I understand *to wax poetic* about something. But *to wax on*? To me, that makes no sense. Even my beloved *New York Times* has begun to abuse the innocent *wax.*

Witness this example from a recent article: 'To families in their prime child-rearing years, all the design magazines *waxing on* about fashion fabrics and the home stores showing off containers disguised as style statements no longer register.' Where will the madness end?"

> I know I've heard and seen *wax on* from reputable sources, and I have the same impression you do that it's another way—surely more polite—of saying "blather on." But only *WNW* defines it: "to speak or express oneself [he *waxed on and on* about his prowess]."

"I've recently seen the word *premiate* used in regard to the selection process of the Aga Khan Award for Architecture, as in 'The Aga Khan Trust for Culture coordinates the Imamat's cultural activities and places a special emphasis on the built environment by *premiating* outstanding achievements through The Award for Architecture.' I gather it means 'identify the winner of a prize after the rigors of a long selection process.' I wonder if *premiate* has occurred elsewhere."

> *Premiate* appears in both of our unabridged dictionaries, the *RHUD* and *W3*—and please note that the edition of *W3* I have dates from 1961. The word is not, however, in any of the other, smaller dictionaries.

And that's it for our twenty questions. None of the seven dictionaries takes the majority position on all of them. But as it turns out, on these questions being part of the majority isn't invariably a good thing. Granted, the dictionaries contain stunning amounts of information, and in many ways each one's attention to detail is mind-boggling. In Merriam-Webster dictionaries (*MWC* and *W3*), for instance, a boldface "swung dash" (~) has a completely different significance from a lightface swung dash (~). In *WNW*'s etymologies the symbols *, <, >, and ? have special meanings. And so on. (Caveat: not all such minutiae are flawlessly replicated on CD-ROM.)

Nevertheless, the dictionaries fail to answer many, many language questions authoritatively. Their creators haven't preemptively thought of every possible way to use their handiwork and precluded misunderstanding. They know this—they will be the first to admit that there simply isn't room in a given dictionary to specify everything that anyone might ever wonder about a word. Furthermore, they're human. We are disappointed but not astonished if an excellent restaurant serves us a middling meal or if a well-edited book or periodical contains an occasional typo. We're forgiving if a dear friend forgets to tell us something we wish we'd known. Why should dictionaries be perfect?

You may recall from Chapter One my high-minded talk about having no opinions and seeking to reflect a consensus—but, clearly, I don't think we all ought to go along with whatever the majority of dictionaries seems to call for. Dictionaries are a place for us to start resolving language problems. Still, it's important to keep in mind that even many of their definite assertions aren't beyond dispute.

Right Up Front

Compounding the problem is that few people take the trouble to make sure they're understanding their dictionary the way it intends to be understood. Much as one of my twenty-questions correspondents was long ago informed by a "grammar instructor" that "one places items *on* a table; one does not place anything *on* a day," every one of us has had oversimplified rules about language imparted to us, by teachers or loved ones or co-workers. And if we were taught how to use a dictionary, those instructions were probably also oversimplified, or even wrong. For instance, were you told that the first spelling given for a word is the preferred one? Sometimes it is, but only sometimes. Were you told that the first definition given is the most significant? Sometimes that's true too. And sometimes not.

It's necessary to study the "front matter"—the annotations and lists and small type explaining what the dictionary-makers thought they were doing—in the dictionary or dictionaries you use. A great deal of it makes for dreary reading, I'll admit: "The word *as* may or may not follow the lightface colon. Its presence (as at [2]*crunch*) indicates that the following subsenses are typical or significant examples. Its absence (as at *sequoia*) indicates that the subsenses which follow are exhaustive" (*MWC*); "Multiple-word entries formed from components that are not entirely assimilated into English, whether or not italicized, are usually syllabified and pronounced in full, even when their component parts are pronounced elsewhere in the book" (the *RHUD*); "Where we have had sufficient evidence from our Corpus that a potential runon in fact has a different pattern of linguistic behavior, that term has been defined fully"(*Enc*).

You may skim. Better yet, go straight to the sample entries and the notes about them. Some of the important things to find out are:

- Where more than one spelling is given—for, say, a word like *ambiance* (*ambience*) or *plaguey* (*plaguy*)—does the dictionary consider one of them to be preferred, or at least more common? Generally, dictionaries that list two variants with *or* between them (*ax* or *axe*) explain that these ought to be regarded as approximately equal variants. So choosing always to go along with the first one, though many people do this, is essentially an arbitrary decision.

But wait! In the two Merriam-Webster dictionaries, although two variants joined by *or* ("*ambience* or *ambiance*," for instance) are considered equal variants, if the variants are presented out of alphabetical order (as those *ambiance*s are), that constitutes a hint that the one printed first is "slightly more common than the second"—just so you'll know. And in all of the dictionaries except *Encarta*, a variant that is presented after *also* ("*lasagna* . . . Also spelled *lasagne*," for instance) is considered an unequal, or secondary, variant. *Enc,* in its front matter, simply declares: "The Dictionary takes note wherever a word has more than one possible spelling variant. Such entries appear in boldface type following their headword." ("Headwords" are the words you look up.) *Enc* refuses to be drawn into any discussion of equal versus secondary variants, and its variants never appear after *also*.

Now, that may seem like enough about spelling, but it's not all there is.

For instance, *NOAD,* just to drive those of us who are looking for guidance completely bonkers—pardon me, to allow us the greatest possible freedom to make our own wise choices—notes:

Hyphenation of noun compounds: There is no hard-and-fast rule to determine whether, for example, *airstream, air stream,* or *air-stream* is correct. All forms are found in use: all are recorded in the Oxford databank and other standard texts. . . . To save space and avoid confusion, only one of the three potential forms of each noun compound (the standard American one) is generally used as the headword form in *The New Oxford American Dictionary*. This does not, however, imply that other forms are incorrect or not used.

And *MWC* says:

Variation in the styling of compound words in English is frequent and widespread. It is often completely acceptable to choose freely among open, hyphenated, and closed alternatives (as *life style, life-style*, or *lifestyle*). However, to show all the stylings that are found for English compounds would require space that can be better used for other information. So this dictionary limits itself to a single styling for a compound: *peacemaker, pell-mell, boom box*. When a compound is widely used and one styling predominates, that styling is shown. When a compound is uncommon or when the evidence indicates that two or three stylings are approximately equal in frequency, the styling shown is based on the analogy of similar compounds.

Read your front matter. You may decide after all to make a habit of using the first, or only, spelling given. It's just that if you occasionally get into arguments about spelling and are inclined to announce huffily "The dictionary gives *my* spelling first," you ought to know whether you're playing fair.

• Where the dictionary gives more than one pronunciation—for, say, *Caribbean* ("*cair*-uh-*bee*-un" or "kuh-*rib*-ee-un") or our friend *ambiance* ("*am*-bee-ens" or "ahn-bee-*ahns*")—does it consider one of them to be preferred, or usual? Probably not. Except that *or* usually doesn't appear between equal variant pronunciations, the story is similar to the one about variant spellings.

Of course, if two or more pronunciations are given and the dictionary doesn't state a preference, those of us with a perfectionist streak may want to know whether one is actually better or best, and if so, why. But for that we'll need to go beyond dictionaries to the more specialized pronunciation resources covered in Chapter Seven.

• Are the definitions for a word given in order of significance? (The *AHD, Enc, NOAD,* and the *RHUD* do this.) Or historical order? (*MWC, WNW,* and *W3* do this.) Parts of speech, however, must be also factored into the order of definitions: when a word, such as *that,* can be more than one part of speech, all of the dictionaries group the meanings for each part of speech together. But it's generally impossible to be strict about grouping meanings by part of speech *and* about presenting the definitions either in order of importance or in historical order. So there's no use reading very much into the order in which definitions are given.

I recall getting a letter from a man who was having a dispute with his wife about the connotations of *inspire.* (You can read the whole story in Chapter Eight.) His wife had defended her point of view by showing him "the eighth or ninth dictionary definition" of the word, he said—his implication being that this couldn't be a common meaning. But since he didn't say what dictionary they were using, I couldn't tell whether the dictionary considered it to be an especially current meaning or a relatively minor one. Unless the dictionary has labeled it *"obsolete,"* *"archaic,"* or the like, it's a recognized, functioning meaning.

- Does the dictionary include proper nouns, such as the names of countries and prominent people? Another of my correspondents once complained that *America* wasn't in his dictionary, and he took this to mean that we shouldn't use *America* to refer to the United States or, presumably, anything else. How awkward! I'll bet he was using *Merriam-Webster's Collegiate,* which doesn't list geographic entities in the main body of the dictionary but gives them separately, in an appendix. Even the main body of *MWC,* though, gives *American* and some two dozen related words or compounds (for instance, *Americana, American plan,* and *American Sign Language*) that aren't geographic entities per se.

- How does the dictionary treat words that its makers believe should be, or often are, capitalized in written American English? Does it show "foreign" words in italics, or has the decision been made that all the words it defines are English and none should be italicized?

- Does it give all common and uncommon "inflections"? That is, does it give plurals for nouns (*inflection: inflections*); past, past-participial, present-participial, and third-person-singular forms of verbs (*give: gave, given, giving, gives*); and comparatives and superlatives for adjectives and adverbs that form them with changes to the word itself, such as *-er* and *-est* endings (*common: commoner, commonest*)? Or does it give only irregular ones? Or only ones for the root words of compounds?

W3, for instance—which you'll recall is unabridged, so you might expect each of its entries to tell you everything about that word—gives the *-s* plural for *bird* under *bird*, but not under *blackbird* or *bluebird* or *bowerbird* or *butcherbird*. A naif who sees the *-s* in some noun entries might suppose that an entry without an *-s* has a plural the same as the singular—like the plurals of *sheep* and *moose*, say. But *W3* does spell out the plurals of *sheep* and *moose*, because *sheep* and *moose* are root words. The front matter explains what's going on.

• What is the dictionary's position on "status" or "usage" or "style level and register" labels? *Enc* and *NOAD* love them, employing, respectively, fifteen and fourteen labels such as "*dated*," "*literary*," "*formal*," "*babytalk*," "*offensive*," and "*taboo*." *W3* employs some labels but is famously wary of using them to make value judgments. *W3*'s front matter says, for instance, "The stylistic label *substand* for 'substandard' indicates status conforming to a pattern of linguistic usage that exists throughout the American language community but differs in choice of word or form from that of the prestige group in that community." And "No word is invariably slang, and many standard words can be given slang connotations or used so inappropriately as to become slang."

Read your front matter.

Plan B

Imagine that you've just bought a new clock radio or telephone answering machine. To set it, would you prefer fiddling with it to reading the manual? If so, thank you for reading the discussion of front matter, and please allow me to describe an alternative method for figuring out most of what a dictionary thinks it's telling you: looking up, in the main body of the dictionary, things you know that are analogous to the things you want to find out.

"I am a copy editor with a seemingly easy question. I am perplexed about the plural form of *foe*. There is no plural form listed in *Merriam-Webster's Collegiate,* and the definitions are all in the singular form. Is the plural form simply *foes?*"

MWC doesn't give plurals when they're regular—as in, just add an -s. To check this, try looking up *antagonist, enemy, opponent,* and *rival,* and you'll see that only in the *enemy* entry is the plural given; it's there because the -y changes to -ies. Yes, the plural of *foe* is *foes.*

"A friend of ours was chastised by another friend while dining at a restaurant. Friend 1 had ordered her steak rare. Upon receiving it, she was disappointed and said she had wanted it *rarer.* Friend 2 (a.k.a. The Critic) stated that that usage was incorrect—that 1 should have said she wanted it *more rare,* and that *rarer* was OK for comparing near-extinct species, perfect diamonds, and the like, but not for the relative doneness of cooked meat.

"Dictionaries we have consulted do not specifically deal with this issue, a fact that (along with our instincts) leads us to believe that 1's usage was just dandy and 2 was being altogether too picky. Please advise."

You're right about 1's usage but mistaken when you say that dictionaries don't cover this. All seven of our dictionaries have separate entries for *rare* meaning things like "near-extinct" and *rare* meaning "lightly cooked," because these two meanings have distinct histories. And both entries in each dictionary give *rarer* and *rarest,* to show that those are the standard comparative and superlative forms.

Please note that if 1 had said she wanted her meat *pinker* and 2 had objected to that, 1 would still have been right but only some dictionaries would have come out and said so by presenting the inflections *pinker* and *pinkest* under the entry *pink.* In English it is regular for one-syllable adjectives and adverbs to add *-er* and *-est,* so most dictionaries don't give these inflections. (*Rarer* is a slightly different case, because the final *e* is dropped when the ending is added.) Similarly, adjectives and adverbs of more than one syllable are regularly, or at least usually, inflected with *more* and *most: more delicious, most delicious.* So dictionaries tend to give comparatives and superlatives for words of more than one syllable only when these do have built-in inflections: *tastier, tastiest.*

"I will share the cost of a hit man for the next reporter who uses either *resonates* or *proactive* in a news story. The dictionary I have consulted gives *resonate* as a verb that can be used in the past tense or as a gerund, but it does not permit *resonates.* As for *proactive,* well, I guess you could be a 'professional active' or you could be 'for active.' Otherwise, I see no use for the word, unless we are ready for *conpassive.*

"P.S. I just noticed that the spell checker on the computer challenged *conpassive* but not *proactive.* Have we gone that far?"

To start with your P.S., yes, we sure have gone that far. Have you looked up *proactive* in a dictionary recently? The only current one that includes so much as a note of caution is *Encarta,* which advises that the word "be used sparingly"—and as it happens, I wrote that note, having often seen *proactive* derided as jargon. But the word has been part of our language since the 1930s, and evidently lots of people find it useful or it wouldn't crop up as much as it does. I'm not saying you have to use it or even like it, but good grief, lighten up!

On to *resonates:* You must have looked *resonate* up in *MWC, NOAD,* the *RHUD,* or *WNW.* These dictionaries don't give the present-tense third-person-singular inflection unless it's irregular. Compare, oh, say, *redound* or *respect* (surely you have nothing against "It *redounds* to a person's credit to be well informed" and "He *respects* educated opinion"?) and you'll see what I mean.

"I was taught that you can create a noun by switching the order of a verb and its object and making the two into a single word. A person who lifts weights is a *weightlifter.* A *schoolteacher* teaches school. When it is time to switch back to the verb, the single word is broken up and the verb comes first, followed by the object. But nowadays the noun becomes a verb and the two pieces are not separated. 'He *schoolteaches.*' 'He *weightlifts.*'

"I don't see *schoolteach* or *weightlift* in my dictionary. Is this now accepted usage?"

Let's look in our unabridged dictionaries, the *RHUD* and *W3:* neither of them gives those verbs, though they do give *weightlifter* and *schoolteacher.* To test the general principles you describe, why don't we try another couple of terms, such as *shotputter* and *shoplifter.* The two dictionaries agree that *shot put* is the event in which shot-putters compete; but to make a verb out of it, you'd say *put the shot.* They agree, too, that *shoplift* as a verb is standard, having been derived from *shoplifter* in the early nineteenth century pretty much the way you describe. The only thing is, a *shoplifter* doesn't lift shops but lifts, or steals, *from* shops. By now it's clear—isn't it?—that the relationship between verbs and compound nouns is more complicated than you've been led to believe.

"Is *wildlife* singular or plural? *Wildlife is abundant* or *wildlife are abundant*?"

Dictionaries answer this, albeit indirectly. Compare *cattle:* dictionaries call it a plural noun or specify that it's used with a plural verb. But all of our dictionaries call *wildlife* simply a noun; this means they consider it singular, and no two ways about it.

A mysterious fact about *wildlife* in dictionaries, however, is that none of the seven specifies that the word's plural is the same as its singular, or gives a plural (would it be the irregular *wildlives,* or would it follow the pattern of *still life* and *still lifes*?), or explains unambiguously in its front matter why no plural is given. This is more an example of what I was warning you about with respect to dictionaries than it is something to remember about *wildlife:* they can't and don't spell out every single thing you might wish they would.

"Since *jack-o'-lantern* is obviously a contraction of *jack of the lantern,* why shouldn't its plural be *jacks-o'-lantern* instead of the ubiquitous *jack-o'-lanterns*?"

You mean the way the plural of *cat-o'-nine-tails* is *cats-o'-nine-tails* and the plural of *will-o'-the-wisp* (which has a meaning in common with *jack-o'-lantern*) is *wills-o'-the-wisp*? But they're not. The plurals are *cat-o'-nine-tails* and *will-o'-the-wisps. Jack-o'-lanterns* and the terms most closely analogous to it take a final *-s* if they don't already have one, as opposed to terms with a spelled-out *of,* such as *captain(s) of the fleet, wave(s) of the future,* and *jack(s)-of-all-trades.*

I'll admit that you'll have one heck of a time using any given dictionary to figure all this out. The only dictionary to give all six of the terms I just named is *W3,* and it specifies the plurals for exactly two of them: *cat-o'-nine-tails* and *jacks-of-all-trades. W3's* front matter includes a twenty-three-part section on plurals, but this provides surprisingly little help in figuring out how to pluralize the remaining four terms, including your *jack-o'-lantern.* Although it describes what to do with "three-word compounds consisting of initial noun plus prepositional phrase hyphenated or open"—namely, "pluralize the initial noun"—it says nothing about four-word ones, such as your *jack of the lantern.* Although it explains that "abbreviations formed by truncation or contraction usually add *-s* without apostrophe," it gives no examples longer than *apt* becoming *apts* and *cap* becoming *caps.*

Does this add up to a recommendation on *W3's* part in favor of *jacks-o'-lantern*? If so, why isn't that form as well as *jacks-of-all-trades* given in the main text? Is *W3* then in favor of *jack-o'-lanterns*—which is, after all, the plural specified by every dictionary that gives one? Maybe so, but it's a stretch to infer that from the front-matter material about abbreviations. I couldn't find anything else relevant—and not for lack of trying.

Hidden in Plain Sight

Again, you can tease much more information out of a dictionary if you're clever about what to look up.

"A co-worker referred me to you. I have been appointed to research the word *halacious* or *hellatious,* meaning 'really horrible, worse than hell.' I recently saw it in a journalist's column as 'It was a *hellatious* smell.' Thus ensued a disagreement about the spelling. I haven't used this word in a long time, but I was always under the impression that it was *hal-* and not *hell-.* I cannot find it in a dictionary; I suggested it might be a made-up word, like *humongous.* Could you please shed some light on this?"

Actually, all seven dictionaries spell the word *hellacious,* which is just distant enough from where an entry for *hellatious* would be that you can miss it if you are intent on finding the latter. Here you might have done better if you'd used a CD-ROM. Six of the seven CD-ROM dictionaries will show you a list of headwords near the one you're typing in, and since the list shows only the headwords and *hellacious* is one to seven entries away from where *hellatious* would be, maybe you would have spotted it. The seventh CD-ROM, *NOAD,* shows you exactly what you request and nothing else. Type in *hellatious* and it will report "No result found." For this reason, any of the other CD-ROMs is more useful for finding words whose spelling you're unsure of.

P.S. All the dictionaries give *humongous,* too, most with *humungous* as a variant.

❖

"I understand some things: 'He is a *one-year-old* baby' is hyphenated. 'The baby is *one year old*' is not hyphenated. But what about 'He is a *one-year-old*'? Or should that be 'He is a *one year old*'? Can you help? When the phrase is used as a noun, I don't know what to do with it."

A meaning given under *old,* noun, in the *AHD* is "An individual of a specified age: *a five-year-old.*" Other current dictionaries give similar definitions, with hyphenated examples; *WNW* even specifies that such compounds are hyphenated.

Usually we can look up a whole word or compound, but sometimes the information we need is given under the entry for a part of it, and not necessarily the first part.

"Is it *food-borne* illness or *foodborne* illness? Please advise."

Try looking under *borne* and then under some other *-borne* words. Only *MWC* and *NOAD* call *borne* an adjective that is used in combination. *MWC,* under *borne,* gives the examples *soilborne* and *airborne,* but (as the CD-ROM makes clear without any special effort on the user's part) it contains separate, hyphenated entries for *tick-borne* and *wind-borne. NOAD,* under *borne,* gives one closed-up and one hyphenated example: *waterborne bacteria* and *insect-borne pollen.* The remaining five dictionaries treat *borne* simply as one of two past participles of *bear* (the other is *born*). None of the dictionaries has an entry for *foodborne,* though all of them have entries for *airborne* and *waterborne.* I would hyphenate *food-borne.*

❖

"In recent months a puzzling word has reared its head once again: *surveil.* When I first heard it used, a few years ago, I assumed that the speaker was simply coining a new form of the word *surveillance,* as in 'We set up a team to *surveil* the suspect's house.' The correct usage, I assumed, would be 'We set up a team to *survey* the suspect's house.' I see, however, that *Merriam-Webster's Collegiate* accepts the word *surveil* as a 'back-formation' of *surveillance.* Are there any other back-formation words in common usage, and are they considered acceptable in standard English?"

Yes, indeed. Back-formations are newer, shorter words created by stripping away affixes (usually endings) from words that entered English with their affixes firmly attached. For instance, *baby-sitter* came to us in that form, and the verb *baby-sit* was derived from it; the verb *laze* is derived from *lazy*, and *edit* from *editor*—as you'll discover if you look up *back-formation* in various dictionaries. As you'd imagine, *surveillance* entered English from French; it did so about two centuries ago, whereas the earliest citation for *surveil* known to *MWC*'s lexicographers is from 1914.

Your reaction to *surveil* is fairly typical of the response people have to a back-formation they aren't used to seeing: they don't quite believe that the thing is a proper word. But *surveil* deserves to be a word, it seems to me, because *survey* threatens to mean a technique of social science or, more likely, land measurement. (See how useful *surveil* is in this recent quotation from *The Philadelphia Inquirer:* "One commando killed a soldier whose job was to *surveil* the border.")

Nonetheless, some other back-formations that were coined long ago have yet to win everyone over. *Burgle,* from *burglar,* is a good example. Though the word has been in use since about 1870, even now *WNW* labels it *"informal"; NOAD* calls it "another term for *burglarize"* and points out that it was originally meant to be humorous. Ultimately, all we have to go on is our own taste. Does a word irritate *us?* Then we should try to find some other way to make our point. If we can't—well, then we've discovered what the word is for.

"A TV commentator recently referred to a new software package as having been *troubleshooted.* Does a suitable past-tense verb exist for something that has undergone a troubleshooting process?"

Here, too, we have a back-formation: *troubleshooter* was the original word. (Though *NOAD* calls *troubleshooter* a derivative of the verb, not even its big sister the *Oxford English Dictionary* agrees.) So the form *troubleshooted* is less crazy than it may sound. *NOAD* fails to specify that the past tense of the verb is irregular, as it does with *overshoot* (*overshot*), and its front matter doesn't tell you to refer to the root verb (*shoot*)— so it seems implicitly to be calling for *troubleshooted.* The *RHUD* actually gives *troubleshooted* as a variant, together with *troubleshot. WNW* doesn't give the verb at all, past, present, or future—only *troubleshooter* and *troubleshooting.* However, the other dictionaries either explicitly or implicitly (as in, *W3*'s front matter does tell you to look under the root verb) are in favor of *troubleshot.*

Curiouser and Curiouser

Nouns and adjectives and back-formations—oh, my! Dictionaries take for granted that their users know at least something about parts of speech and other grammatical concepts. Nowadays this may be unwise of them, because schools have paid little attention to traditional grammar for some decades, and grammar has never been a discipline that's easy to pick up on your own. Nonetheless, do bear in mind that dictionaries define *noun* and *adjective* and *back-formation* (the *RHUD* prefers the unhyphenated form *back formation*) and other grammar-related terms, in case you're a bit hazy on what some of them mean.

If you are hazy, there's no shame in it. So I don't exactly hold it against people who send me letters betraying deeply strange ideas about words and grammar. Certainly, sensible and well-informed people write me too, often after they've bumped up against aspects of the language that are strange.

"Would you be so kind to settle a dispute I have with my employer, a hospital, regarding their improper use of the word *none*? As a laboratory technician, I report many test results on standardized forms. One form that is used by the parasitology department indicates test results. In the event that parasites are absent in a given sample, a box marked *none seen* is to be checked. I have objected to the use of *none seen* for twenty years. *None* is a pronoun meaning 'nobody, no one, no man' and does not refer to worms, since worms are not human.

"Do you agree that the proper wording of the selection should be *nothing observed, parasites not present,* or something else? I anxiously await your reply."

But *it* is a pronoun, and that can refer to a worm. And *they* is a pronoun, and that can refer either to people or to worms. And *that,* too, is a pronoun, which can refer to a person or a worm.

None (ahem) of our seven dictionaries contradicts the idea that *none* can mean "not any" of something nonhuman.

"There is an increase in the occurrence of the word *intentioned*. For example, when describing people who hope their actions will result in good being done, it is said they are *well intentioned*. Shouldn't the word be *intended*? Isn't *well* an adverb? *Intention* is a noun. *Intend* is a verb. Nouns have no past tense! I may *have* intentions, but I cannot *intention*!"

Sorry, but what ever made you think English as it has been handed down to us over the ages is as orderly and logical as all that? About four centuries ago *intention* and also *intent* were verbs, together with *intend*. The verb *intention* has left traces of itself in the contemporary adjective *well-intentioned* (which, like other *well-* compounds, appears with a hyphen in dictionaries but is not ordinarily hyphenated in text unless it is placed before a noun). *Well-intentioned* appears in all seven of our dictionaries, though *W3* covers it not under *well-* but under *intentioned,* an adjective that, *W3* specifies, is "often used in combination."

"The use—or, as I see it, misuse—of *thinly* in constructions like *thinly sliced* bothers me. I cannot conceive of a *thinly* this way. Shouldn't it be *thin sliced* or, better, *sliced thin*? It seems to me that the misuse describes the actions of the slicer rather than the results."

You're quite right that *thin-sliced* is considered better form than *thinly sliced*. But *thin* here is the very same part of speech as *thinly,* each of them being an adverb, according to all of our dictionaries. As the *AHD* explains it, one of the meanings of the adverb *thin* is "so as to be thin." Go figure. But in fact many adverbs have two forms (*thinly* and *thin, thickly* and *thick, quickly* and *quick*), the terser of which is standard in combinations: *thick-cut, quick-acting.*

Some of the most interesting language questions turn on what part of speech a given word is or how it was derived. As these grow subtler, dictionaries become less helpful and other books, such as usage manuals, more so. Dictionaries will tell you that, say, *that* can be a pronoun, an adjective, an adverb, and a conjunction (*W3* will tell you it's a noun as well, in a phrase like "Squire This and Farmer *That*"), and they'll probably give you a few examples of the word doing each of those jobs. Usage manuals will devote whole paragraphs or pages to any of these parts of speech that tend to give people trouble.

Distinctions and Differences

One more use to which people often put dictionaries is distinguishing between similar terms. Some people, and some dictionaries with some words, do this more successfully than others.

"My pet peeve regarding Americanization of the English language happens to be *acclimate.* For example, 'This dog was *acclimated* at 40,000 feet.' The word is *acclimatized,* although *Webster's* identifies *acclimate* as a word and, in its most recent edition grudgingly included it as a synonym of *acclimatize*—identical. Problem: It is most often mispronounced as 'acclamate' and, therefore, if the word existed at all, would mean 'acclaim' or 'hold in high regard.'

"I just about fell over when I saw it on my dog's vaccination verifying her medical soundness for flight when she arrived here from Washington State. I thought, 'What did they do, have a little award party for her up there or something?' I had to search my dictionary—*Oxford* of course—for this weird word.

"I had major fights with an old boyfriend who used it liberally when talking about *acclamating* to certain southern destinations during his world travels. Yuck!!! He was *supposed* to be a 'Hollywood screenwriter.'

"Two words: one real, one made up. The second makes for real confusion and completely unnecessary nonsense when a perfectly good, easily recognizable word already exists. But then I guess that would only bother someone like me. Irregardless of current convention. Grrrr!!"

Yes, *acclimatize* and *acclimate* are synonyms. But *acclimate* dates from the late eighteenth century and *acclimatize* from about forty-five years later—so what's the big deal? Please also note that none of our seven dictionaries gives *acclamate*. The word *is* in the *Oxford English Dictionary,* which calls it an *"obsolete"* and *"rare"* synonym of *acclaim.* I don't mean to say that there's anything wrong with *acclimatize;* feel free to use it if you wish. And I have no opinion about whether you would have done better to be less combative with your old boyfriend. But for heaven's sake, cut *acclimate,* and your dog's vet, some slack. Regardless.

"My current pet peeve is all the talk about priestly *celibacy.* That word does not mean 'abstinence from sexual activity'—that's *chastity*!—but rather 'unmarried.' In fact abstinence from sexual activity is the conclusion of a syllogism whose major premise is: Sexual activity is morally permissible only within the sacred bonds of marriage. Priests must never marry (that is, they must be and remain *celibate*). Therefore, a priest is not morally permitted to engage in sexual activity. After saying so, however, I'm the first to concede that this is a lost cause. *Everyone*—not just Joe Six-Pack—now equates celibacy with chastity, which it ain't."

You're right about the words' history, and right, too, that everyone—by which I mean each of our seven dictionaries—allows the two words considerable overlap in meaning. Here's the story as told in a usage note in the *AHD:*

Historically, *celibate* means only "unmarried"; its use to mean "abstaining from sexual intercourse" is a 20th-century development. But the new sense of the word seems to have displaced the old, and the use of *celibate* to mean "unmarried" is now almost sure to invite misinterpretation in other than narrowly ecclesiastical contexts. Sixty-eight percent of the Usage Panel rejected the older use in the sentence *He remained celibate* [unmarried], *although he engaged in sexual intercourse.*

Just for an analogy: In the 1920s the word *jazz* meant, among other things, what people who are celibate and chaste don't do. That meaning has pretty much gone by the wayside by now. Why fight it if the meaning of *celibacy* you once learned goes that way too?

"At the hospital where I work, the purchasing and supply department was originally called the Materials Management department. Several years ago, when they started cooperative purchasing efforts with other area hospitals, they changed the name to *Materiel* Management. Now I am appalled to see the department being called *Ma-teriels* Management and staff being called *materiels* coordinators.

"I'm not the best with grammar, but it seems to me that there are two errors with *materiels*—the first being the connotation and the second being the plural form. Several other secretaries within the organization have questioned people in the department about this word usage; however, the response has been negative. I'm hoping that you could give us something authoritative."

If the high muckamuck responsible for that name looked *materiel* up in *MWC,* he or she would have found it spelled *matériel* or *materiel,* but the definition would have been, simply, "equipment, apparatus, and supplies used by an organization or institution"—which seems apt enough. Three other dictionaries give a meaning like that but then go on to say something like this (the quotation is from *WNW*): "specifically, weapons, equipment, supplies, etc. of armed forces: distinguished from *personnel.*" The three remaining dictionaries give the military meaning only. The military sense is the original one in English, and it's the sole sense that some reputable sources still recognize. So I agree with you that applying the word to hospital supplies—of all things—is inappropriate.

You and your fellow secretaries are also right that no more than we should talk about *personnels* ought anyone to use the word *materiel* in the plural, except under circumstances so special that I can't imagine them. Yet *W3* says the word has an inflected form ending with *-s.* Leave the *AHD, Enc,* or *NOAD* lying open on the offending muckamuck's desk? These are the dictionaries that give only the military meaning, and none of them gives a plural. You and I know that this latter fact doesn't mean what the uninitiated might think—but I won't tell if you won't.

❖

"The subject of my concern is pervasive and fast-growing: the practice of combining noun and adjective into one word, which often has quite a different meaning from the original combination. Consider *back seat,* referring of course to the seat behind the driver in an automobile. Its associate *backseat* is (or was) an adjective, commonly used in the phrase *backseat driver.* Nowadays, however, only the formerly adjectival form is used to describe that location in the car, leaving me, at least, waiting in vain for the noun to arrive which it supposedly modifies. There is no such noun as *backseat.* Another obvious example is *back yard* and *backyard.*"

I happen to share your preference for the two-word nouns and one-word adjectives, because *backseat* and *backyard* look to me as if they should be pronounced the way *backache* and *backbone* and *backdrop* and *backgammon* and most other *back-* compounds are: with the accent on the first syllable. That is the way they are pronounced when they're used as adjectives: "A *back*seat driver sits in the back *seat.*" But none of the dictionaries agrees with us on all four forms. Of our seven dictionaries, four consider *back seat* to be the usual noun. None mentions *backseat* as an adjective (or attributive noun), though *Enc* and *WNW* give *back-seat* instead. All the dictionaries except *Enc* consider *backyard* to be the usual or only noun form for this word, and just three mention an adjectival or attributive use.

Most dictionaries assert that they give or prefer the forms they do because these forms are standard, or at least are appreciably more common than other variants. One way or the other with respect to *back seat* versus *backseat* as a noun, about half of our dictionaries have got to be wrong. What's standard in the other cases is none too clear, either. For once, it's a good thing we have opinions!

❖

"At the company where I work, there is a link on one of our intranet Web pages for checking items currently in stock. This is connected directly to the inventory database. When the stock level of an item drops to zero, the item is instantly removed from the list. This may happen twice a day or twice a week. Is this list being updated *continuously* or *continually*? I've been told that *continuously* is grammatically incorrect.

"According to my dictionary, *continual* is an action without cessation and *continuous* pertains to things that are uninterrupted, like connected sheets of paper. However, an example given under continuous is that 'creation is a continuous process.' These definitions don't seem to point to one clear choice. *Continuously* seems correct to me. Please help."

Your dictionary isn't doing a good job of explaining the traditional distinction between the two words. Here's what the *AHD* has to say: "*Continual* is chiefly restricted to what is intermittent or repeated at intervals: *The continual banging of the shutter in the wind gave me a headache. Continuous* implies lack of interruption: *The horizon is a continuous line.*"

The "without cessation" in your dictionary's definition is what's misleading you, I suspect. Anything that happens "twice a day or twice a week" is *continual;* anything that is happening constantly (if your computers stay on all night, their connection to the intranet might be an example) is *continuous.*

❖

"I often see the word *jell* in print, used in the context of a group's chemistry having *jelled* or a team having *jelled*. However, I am also seeing it spelled *gel*. For example, one recent Sunday evening a Washingtonpost.com story about an NFL game bore the headline 'Washington's Offense Finally *Jells* in the Second Half'; the next morning the headline for the same story read 'Offense *Gels* as Washington Rolls to Second Win.' Who had it right—the night shift or the Monday-morning crew?"

It's a rare Monday-morning quarterback who gets it wrong, but evidently you've found one who did. Though the two words share an etymology, *jell* is much more common in figurative senses like the ones you describe, as all of our dictionaries except *Enc* and the *RHUD* suggest or state.

"Is there a usage difference between the terms *thought-provoking* and *provocative*? You will hear the two used interchangeably in the press and in conversation. I feel that the term *provocative* carries undertones of incendiarism or sexuality. In contrast, *thought-provoking* just means the topic is conducive to further reflection. Perhaps this interpretation is too specific and limiting?"

Only in *Enc* and *NOAD* will you find *thought-provoking* per se defined; it means, according to the latter, "stimulating careful consideration or attention: *thought-provoking questions.*" Because *provoking* alone tends to mean, as the *AHD* puts it, "troubling the nerves or peace of mind, as by repeated vexations: *a provoking delay at the airport,*" you won't find a sensible answer to this question in the other dictionaries unless you already know the answer and are willing to read between the lines.

It's quite true that *provocative* often implies the provocation of things other than reflection. But whether lascivious images or, say, epistemological concepts are being provoked is a matter for the reader or hearer—and the context—to decide. I wouldn't go so far as to call *provocative* wrong where it means *thought-provoking;* it's just less specific. Only where the meaning is ambiguous (as it is, for instance, in "Angelina Jolie's *provocative* new interpretation of Kant's *Critique of Pure Reason*") is using *provocative* a bad idea.

In short, dictionaries can solve a wide range of language problems—as possibly you already knew. No dictionary, however, can be trusted to solve all of them definitively. Then, too, it's easy to misinterpret or overinterpret what the dictionary is saying.

Often we'll need other kinds of language references to find out what we want to know. But before we look into those, let's choose a dictionary that suits you, so that we can get out of the maddening habit of looking everything up seven times.

CHAPTER THREE

Getting the Answers You Want

What would the perfect dictionary be like? None of the dictionaries in existence is perfect, so we'll need to imagine the range of features we want. Let's think big.

- Ideally, a dictionary should contain all the words we're likely to come across in everyday situations, so if we look something up and don't find it, that will tell us something more than that our dictionary is heavily abridged or out of date. Then again, the perfect dictionary wouldn't contain every possible bit of information about every possible word, because the answers to common questions would get buried in the avalanche of specialized vocabulary and minutiae.

    Most "words" that dictionaries define are unitary concepts—hence the separate entries you'll see for *word, word of mouth, word processor,* and so forth. But the number of unitary concepts available to us even in everyday use is infinite: consider *one, two, three, . . . one hundred and one, one hundred and two, one hundred and three, . . . one billion and one, one billion and two, one billion and three, . . . one hundred trillion and one . . .* Obviously, the ideal dictionary's editors need to make judicious choices about what to include and what to leave out.

- A dictionary should be current. It should include the new words and expressions, and the new meanings for old words, that we wonder about. For instance, is *brick-and-mortar*—an adjective to describe the kind of store you can walk or drive to, as opposed to Internet-only stores—in standard use now? Or does it chiefly turn up as jargon in specialized contexts like marketing reports? As an abbreviation for *business-to-business,* describing businesses that sell to one another, not consumers, which is preferred: *B2B* or *B-to-B* or *b-to-b*? In whatever form, is the abbreviation in standard use? Is *buff* established as an adjective having to do with physique? What about *disconnect* as a noun: "a *disconnect* between his brain and his mouth"? Is *email* or *e-mail* or *E-mail* the usual form nowadays? What kind of haircut is a *mullet*? Is *spam* slang or standard when it means unsolicited e-mail? What about *spam* as a verb? And since the reference is ultimately to Spam™ luncheon meat, should the conscientious citizens among us avoid the word, so as not to encroach on Spam's trademark?

As we saw in Chapter Two, up-to-date dictionaries do answer questions like these, or at least they provide us with a basis on which to answer them. Naturally, we don't want a dictionary to be just making things up; we want it to supply us with information determined by real-world research—and all of them oblige us, in one way or another. The most old-fashioned lexicographic method employs drawer after drawer of index cards of citations that have been copied out by sharp-eyed readers and filed alphabetically, so that they're ready to be sorted and extrapolated from. The latest method employs electronic corpora (that's the plural of *corpus*). Linguistic corpora consist of millions of words of text from newspapers, books, journals, pamphlets, transcripts of conversations and of radio and television programs, and miscellaneous other sources of words in context. Type *spam*, for instance, into a computer linked to a linguistic corpus, and line after line of text, each containing *spam*, will fill your screen, kind of like this:

… for nearly 60 years over **Spam** and eggs to talk about …

… surfing and improved anti-**spam** and parental controls, as it …

… probably being promoted by **spam** e-mail. Here's a …

… nuisance to telemarketers and **spam** e-mail. "I …

… infomercials, Web sites, **spam** e-mails and a 28-page …

… Michigan's proposed anti-**spam** legislation is still moving …

… e-mail address on a do-not-**spam** list within the Department …

… cherry tomatoes, baby bibs, **Spam** sandwiches, key chains, …

… allows users to configure **Spam** settings and view the …

… On the rare occasion where a **spam** slips thru, SpamFighters …

… also would require senders of **spam** to register with the state …

… will they barbecue? Pheasant? **Spam**? Tofurkey? …

The citations here appear with the words immediately following *spam* in alphabetical order, but users of a corpus can re-sort them in various ways. And for any given citation, more of the context is only a click or two away.

To an extent, we can be our own lexicographers, because tools now publicly available on the Internet allow us to verify what dictionaries report about current usage. The list above, for example, is drawn not from a corpus proper but from two of these publicly available databases and search engines. So we can check dictionaries' work, finding out for ourselves how speakers of American English (or other varieties of English) use the language, both in professionally edited media and in the word world at large. Chapter Four, and to some extent later chapters, will discuss the range and depth of ways that Internet resources can be useful to us who care about words. For our purposes here, I've used Internet tools to research some questions about newish terms which dictionaries also answer.

It's a fact, for example, that *brick-and-mortar* often appears in mainstream newspapers and magazines without a "gloss," or explanation; that *B2B* (or, less commonly, *b-to-b* or *B-to-B*) appears in business contexts but rarely ventures outside them unglossed; that *buff* in the sense of "physically toned" is known unto such mainstream media outlets as CNBC News, *The Arizona Republic,* and *People* magazine; that the noun *disconnect* is mainstream too; that *e-mail* is vastly more common than *email* or *E-mail,* particularly in professionally edited writing; that *mullet* as a word for a haircut that's short in front and long in back is well known to journalists and pop-culture hobbyists alike; and that no matter how Hormel Foods might feel about it, *spam* in reference to e-mail, as a noun and as a verb, is likewise widespread and standard.

Knowing such things, as we all can do, gives us a way to judge which dictionaries really are current.

- A dictionary should accommodate the diversity of America and its points of view. By this I mean not just political correctness and multiculturalism but also historical and conservative usage. For instance, it seems to me, a good dictionary should note that *nigger* is now highly offensive in general use; that African Americans using the word among themselves only rarely intend it as an insult; and that the word did turn up in polite general discourse in the past—we needn't lump Joseph Conrad with the Ku Klux Klan for having written a book titled *The Nigger of the 'Narcissus.'* Much the same goes for *girl* as used in reference to women. *Chairman, fireman,* and *policeman* are increasingly démodé, but so is *chairperson*—and *fireperson* and *policeperson* are nonstarters. What words are people using instead?

  It's also the case that for the past few years *Mumbai* has been the official name of what was formerly known as *Bombay,* India. Even the U.S. State Department calls the city Mumbai, but because this remains news to many nondiplomats, a good dictionary should contain both names, cross-referenced. And we mustn't allow ourselves to discriminate against the chic: the Caribbean island of St. Barthélemy ought to be in the dictionary too. Actually, you'd think the name used by people who take vacations there, *St. Bart's*—or would that be *St. Bart* or *St. Barts* or *Saint Barth* or whatever?—also ought to be included, but none of our dictionaries gives a short form.

Muslims are likely to take offense if they are called *Mohammedans;* Asians may feel similarly about being called *Orientals;* and I promise you that not everybody knows such things, so the information should be noted. People with schizophrenia, people who work with them, and their family members may dislike it when *schizophrenic* is used to mean, simply, "erratic" or "contradictory." If someone wants to offend someone else, OK—that's one of the many ways to interact which language affords us. But when people ruffle feathers out of ignorance and then wonder what's the matter with the person they've insulted, it's ridiculous—and dictionaries have a role to play in preventing such misunderstandings.

- A dictionary should make clear not only how words and phrases are used but also which common expressions and constructions brand their users as barbarians in word mavens' eyes. It should, for instance, discuss whether to use *a* or *an* before words like *heroic* and *historic.* It should explain the traditional distinction between *compare to* and *compare with,* preferably without insisting that everyone observe it, since not even every well-spoken person does. It should define *impact* as a verb that's used figuratively (as in "This word *impacts* the mind strongly"), meanwhile pointing out that plenty of people shrink from *impact* when it's used in reference to anything but physical collisions. It should point out that *irregardless* is nonstandard but that people who know this sometimes use it jocularly—the same way educated people sometimes say *ain't.* A dictionary should note that the nouns *data* and *media* are traditionally plural but that nowadays some reputable sources do use them, in particular senses, with singular verbs. It should make clear that not only *Spam* but also *Kleenex* and *Styrofoam* and *Xerox* are trademarks, and *Laundromat* is a service mark (like a trademark, only for services), and it should preferably also at least hint at—with a comment like "often occurs in print in lowercase" or by presenting the initial letter as "usually" lowercase—which of these marks are often encroached on.

- A dictionary should give not just etymologies but also approximate dates of when words entered English, and if the word's history is interesting or widely misunderstood, it should provide information about that.

- A dictionary should be the product of ongoing research under stable direction. So many words of English are spoken and written nowadays that one could probably assemble a dictionary's worth of citations out of the newspapers, magazines, journals, and books published, the Web pages created, and transcripts of the television and radio programs broadcast, and the conversations held in any given week. But that would give disproportionate importance to the buzzwords then current and, through sheer randomness, would probably result in the omission of a few culturally significant things, such as, oh, say, *Monticello* and *salary*—neither of which, as it happens, appears in the print edition of the *Encarta World English Dictionary*. (The current CD-ROM and the *Microsoft Encarta College Dictionary* have filled in these gaps.)

- A dictionary should ideally have the weight of some major institutions behind it. For instance, the *Associated Press Style-*

book, The New York Times Manual of Style and Usage, and *The Wall Street Journal Guide to Business Style and Usage* all endorse *Webster's New World.* So hundreds of newspapers use *WNW*'s definitions and spellings, and if we read newspapers every day, we may find *WNW*'s preferences familiar and intuitive. But *The Chicago Manual of Style,* which is widely used in publishing and academia, and *The Gregg Reference Manual,* a stylebook especially popular in the business world, endorse *Merriam-Webster's Collegiate.* So thousands of copy editors and academics and businesspeople will prefer its spellings and definitions. Do you hope—or fear—that the mighty weight of Microsoft, as it's brought to bear on our entire culture by Microsoft Word's spell checker, lies behind *Encarta* and its spellings? It doesn't: the spell checker and the dictionary were developed separately.

- The perfect dictionary should come as a printed book together with a CD-ROM, and the two should correspond closely. The print edition should be inviting, attractive, and easy to use. It should be chock-a-block with color illustrations and diagrams and maps and photographs. Its pronunciations should be readily understandable, and the pronunciation key should be easy to find—perhaps appearing somewhere on every two-page spread.

- The CD-ROM should dazzle us with its wonders. It should pronounce words out loud. When a word is cross-referenced— as when *possum* refers us to *opossum*—clicking on the cross- reference should summon up the other word, rather than amounting to a suggestion that we type it in ourselves. In fact, it's nice if clicking on any word in a definition takes us to the entry for that word. And what fun if the CD-ROM can also give us anagrams (*spam* = *amps, maps,* and *samp*) and rhymes (*am, cam, clam, cram, dam, damn, dram* . . .), and if it allows us to conduct various searches, including ones involving wildcards, or symbols that stand for omitted letters. For instance, what *are* all the words that end in *-gry*? The CD-ROM of *MWC* gives only *angry* and *hungry; W3* gives *aggry* and *anhungry* as well; the *OED* gives many more; and in Chapter Four we'll answer the riddle according to which exactly three such words exist.

We should be able to link the dictionary to Microsoft Word and other programs, so that clicking on a word in text will summon up the dictionary entry for that word. And when we present a CD-ROM with a misspelled word, it should suggest a correctly spelled alternative—say, *desiccate* instead of *dessicate, desirable* instead of *desireable, misspell* instead of *mispell.*

Seven Morphs

If all of that is the ideal, how close does each of our dictionaries come? To find out, for one last time I looked up an awful lot of stuff in septuplicate—hundreds of terms, including but not limited to the questions and desiderata presented above. Is a plural given for *crème brûlée?* Is one of the definitions given for *ecstasy* "illegal drug" or the like? Is *the whole enchilada* defined? Is *sniglet?* Are a few versions of the name of the dictator of Libya given, under *Gadhafi, Qaddafi,* or *Gaddafi,* which according to the Nexis database are by far the front-runners? Is a distinction drawn between *analog* and *analogue*? Is the traditional stricture against using *due to* as a preposition explained or at least implied? Stuff like that.

I knocked myself out trying to gather information that was as nearly current as possible, but the darned dictionaries keep changing. *MWC* and *WNW*, for instance, are updated each year. Dictionaries generally undergo modest emendations from one "copyright printing" to the next, to correct any little slip-ups that have been discovered and to add important new words. *Encarta* drove me crazy, because only the *Microsoft Encarta College Dictionary,* which has been revised and condensed from the original *Encarta World English Dictionary,* is available in print in this country, while the current CD-ROM (or DVD) is a tidied-up but not condensed *World English Dictionary* which can be bought only as part of the annually updated Encarta Reference Library.

So please bear in mind that certain specifics about certain dictionaries may have changed if this book is not brand new when you read it. But dictionaries usually evolve rather than change fundamentally. And the principles of what to watch for, and the method for choosing the dictionary that will best suit you as I describe it at the end of this chapter, should apply whenever you're ready to go dictionary shopping.

❖

Of the seven dictionaries, the only one I definitely do not recommend is *Webster's Third New International Dictionary.* The nicest thing I can say about it—sorry!—is that reportedly *Webster's Fourth* will be coming along within the next few years. I have a copy of *W3*'s first printing, from 1961, and I have the latest edition on CD-ROM. And in either format the thing is an antique: no *brick-and-mortar,* no *B2B,* no *buff* physiques, no definition other than "disconnecting switch" given for *disconnect,* noun. *W3* does give *email,* but here is how it's defined: "1: enamel. 2: a moderate bluish green to greenish blue that is lighter than gendarme, deeper than cyan blue, and duller than parrot blue—called also *bleu Louise.*" Say what?

As for diversity and multiculturalism, one of five meanings that both the print edition and the CD-ROM give for the noun *nigger* is "a: Negro" and "b: a member (as an East Indian, a Filipino, an Egyptian) of any very darkskinned race"—and these usages are labeled *"usually taken to be offensive."* The label is not applied, though, to any of the other four meanings given for *nigger,* namely "any of several dark-colored insect larvae," "cotton spinner," "a steam-operated capstan for warping river steamboats over snags and shallows," and "a long-toothed power-propelled lever arm used to position logs on a carriage (as in a sawmill)." What's more, there are separate entries for *nigger chaser,* "a small firework that shoots about on the ground"; *nigger heaven,* "*slang,* the highest balcony or row of seats in a theater"; and *nigger-shooter,* which is defined without commentary as "slingshot." Eesh!

Compared with that, what *W3* says about *girl* is pretty funny:

1 a : a female child <announced the birth of a *girl*> <a study of the performance of primary-school boys and *girls*> b : a young unmarried woman : maiden <a *girl* of striking beauty> c : a single or married woman of any age <gossipy old *girls* of about seventy —J.B.Clayton>
2 a (1) : a female servant : maid <the *girl* brought in and cleared away the dishes —Flora Thompson> (2) : a female employee (as a secretary) <I'll get my *girl* to have a look through the card index —Nevil Shute> b : prostitute c : sweetheart <took his *girl* to the movies> d : daughter <entered his *girl* at a fashionable school>

See what I mean about its being an antique? Another shortcoming is that *W3* doesn't include proper nouns, not even in an appendix, so it's useless if you're trying to figure out how to spell *Muammar al-Qaddafi* or *St. Barthélemy*. Yet another shortcoming is that in its reluctance to make value judgments, it gives more than its share of bad advice. Want to know how to use *ain't*?

1 a : are not <you *ain't* going> <they *ain't* here> <things *ain't* what they used to be> b : is not <it *ain't* raining> <he's here, *ain't* he> c : am not <I *ain't* ready> though disapproved by many and more common in less educated speech, used orally in most parts of the United States by many cultivated speakers especially in the phrase *ain't* I
2 *substandard* a : have not <I *ain't* seen him> <you *ain't* told us> b : has not <he *ain't* got the time> <*ain't* the doctor come yet>

In my circles, that's not *comme il faut.* Granted, lots of people who aren't racist or gaga or slapdash use *W3* as a backup for *Merriam-Webster's Collegiate:* if a word isn't in *MWC,* they look it up in *W3.* (Supposing you use a Mac computer, by this point do you even care that *W3,* along with *MWC,* is available for the Mac platform as well as for Windows?) It makes sense, if you like *MWC,* to remain within the family for your unabridged dictionary—but . . . Merriam-Webster? Could you please hurry up with *Webster's Fourth*?

❖

Unfortunately, I can't recommend the other unabridged dictionary, the *Random House Webster's,* with much enthusiasm. The *RHUD* is fine in all respects except a crucial one: In 2001, shortly after the current, second edition was published, the Random House dictionary division laid off ten lexicographers and shelved all new projects. (Apart from some technological changes to make the companion

CD-ROM compatible with newer Windows platforms, a 2003 edition of the *RHUD* is identical to the one published in 2001, which was an awful lot like the one published in 1998. The CD-ROM doesn't even contain the dictionary's front matter. To me, this omission strongly suggests that no Random House executive has been taking these products seriously for some time.) So the *RHUD* is not being updated, at least not continually or in-house. This dictionary has an excellent lineage and tradition, and it's a shame to let it all go. But the fact that we can't count on its staying current means that it will inevitably sink into irrelevance.

Language professionals such as writers and editors, and to some extent all dictionary users, invest not just money and shelf space but time and mental energy in a dictionary. We become accustomed to the fact that a dictionary gives "foreign" words in italics (as the *RHUD* does), or puts them in an appendix (as *MWC* does), or defines only words that its makers consider to be part of English. Over time we discover whether the people who wrote the usage notes are generally more or less permissive than we are. And we come to an opinion about whether the editors are knowledgeable and bursting with the latest information, or whether they seem to be dully conveying received wisdom. Have the people writing the entries been given enough space to share everything they think is relevant, or does it seem they've been told to cut to the chase? Have parts of the dictionary that in their traditional versions can be tedious to use (I'm thinking particularly of pronunciations and etymologies) been rethought to meet the needs of users today? Have these parts become maybe a little too avant-garde for our taste?

Much as we can get to know a particular movie reviewer until we're able to tell from a review whether we'll enjoy the movie even when we're sure to disagree with the assessment, we get to know our dictionary's makers. And having gone through all that—and committed to memory how the dictionary spells controversial words, what it hyphenates or doesn't, what the symbols it uses mean—we may hope that we'll be able to stick with our dictionary and its successors for life, unless our relationship with it turns really sour. My relationship with the *RHUD* at present is perfectly cordial, but since it is refusing to make a long-term commitment, so am I.

❖

In early 2002 I evaluated for copy editors' purposes what were at the time the current CD-ROM versions of dictionaries. On the 100-point scale I devised, *The New Oxford American Dictionary* earned the highest score, besting the *RHUD* by one point, 60 to 59. That test included more trademarks and proper nouns than probably anyone except copy editors would care about. It paid no attention whatsoever to pronunciations, etymologies, or anything about the print dictionary that didn't carry over onto the CD-ROM. And it was excruciatingly quantitative. None of that, however, can take away from the fact that *NOAD* (published in 2001) is nicely up to date, good on diversity-related issues, and informative about the traditions that adhere to *compare, impact, media,* and so on. It is an attractive book containing many illustrations, photos, and maps (unfortunately not in color), and it also includes a sufficiency of usage notes, synonymies, word histories, and little backgrounders on "specialist vocabulary" from *Achaean* and *acid* to *Zoroastrianism* and *Zulu.*

Its CD-ROM version works in a unique way, appearing as a tiny window either constantly present on your screen or readily available to be summoned from "sleep." You can type words you want to know about into the window, click on them in text, or in some cases simply run your cursor over them. This unusual pop-up-window format is, I suspect, something most people will either love or hate. I—well, I'm afraid I lean toward hating it, because it doesn't allow for browsing, and because it's pitiless. If you're looking up a misspelled word, it will keep telling you "No result found" until you spell the word corectly . . . uh, correctly . . . uh, right.

❖

What I've been calling *Enc* is, again, on paper the *Microsoft Encarta College Dictionary,* first edition (2001), the most substantial Encarta dictionary now in print in the United States; and on CD-ROM the *Encarta World English Dictionary* that comes with the *Encarta Africana,* atlas, encyclopedia, thesaurus, and other materials in the Microsoft Encarta Reference Library. That I wrote a few of the usage notes and vetted others no doubt colors my perceptions of this dictionary. All the same, by objective standards (as in, does it define *b-to-b* and *the whole enchilada* and things like that? yes, indeed) it's relatively up to date.

Enc is famously—some would say notoriously—politically correct. Here, for instance, are its definitions of *girl:*

1. female child: a human female from birth until the age at which she is considered an adult
2. young woman: a young woman (*often considered offensive*)
3. any woman: a woman of any age, especially one who is a friend, a contemporary, or younger than the speaker (*informal*) (*often considered offensive*) • *a night out with the girls*
4. daughter: somebody's daughter, especially when a child (*informal*)
5. girlfriend: a man's or boy's girlfriend

6. way of addressing woman: used as a friendly, intimate, or patronizing form of address to a woman (*offensive in some contexts*)

7. offensive term: an offensive term referring to a young woman servant or employee (*dated*)

8. female creature: a female animal or other creature, especially a young one (*informal*) (*often before nouns*) • *a girl kitten*

And there's a usage note as well, just to let you know that the word can seem disrespectful or patronizing in certain contexts.

Overall, though, it's a plus that *Enc* contains an exceptionally large number of usage notes; these cover traditional grammatical issues as well as diversity-related matters. And the print dictionary features a couple of nifty innovations. There are entries for common misspellings, in which the incorrect headword (for instance, *mispelling*) appears in gray with a line through it and the user is referred to the correct spelling. And there are "Spellcheck" notes for correctly spelled words often misused. For instance, under *grille* it suggests, "See *grill.*" Thank you! Let's hope people do look this one up!

The print edition is light on illustrations and photographs; this is one case in which the CD-ROM (or DVD) has much better visuals, because of the interconnection with the encyclopedias and atlas. If you want to have just the dictionary available on your computer, however, pretty much the same one is available free online at dictionary.msn.com. This is good news for Mac users, since the Encarta Reference Library is available for the Windows platform only (surprise!). Still, a CD-ROM dictionary installed on a hard drive is inherently faster, more flexible, and easier to use than an online one.

❖

At this writing, *Merriam-Webster's Collegiate* is the dictionary that has most recently been substantially revised; the eleventh edition was published in the summer of 2003. If you have a Mac computer and want to use a CD-ROM dictionary, *MWC* is definitely your best bet, for this CD-ROM, unlike most, works for the Mac as well as the Windows platform. In fact, *MWC* is not a bad bet for anyone: it's America's best-selling dictionary. (The press kit that reviewers received about the eleventh edition, I must say, wasn't exactly clear about whether "best-selling" meant just lately or over the dictionary's hundred-plus-year history.) Not only does the relatively inexpensive print edition of *MWC* come with a CD-ROM included, but also it gives buyers a year's subscription to a premium Web site that contains the dictionary, its companion thesaurus and encyclopedia, and a Spanish-English dictionary. (The free, accessible-to-anyone Merriam-Webster Web site at www.m-w.com contains the tenth edition of *MWC*.)

And now *MWC* includes *barista* and *Botox*, *bubkes* and *funplex*, *identity theft* and *nanoscale* and *psyops*—none of which I was able to find in any other current dictionary, though each of these words (an online news database tells me) regularly appears in print. From some word mavens' point of view, however, there is and has long been a problem with *MWC*. Like other Merriam-Webster language products, it is steadfastly descriptive—as in, this is what people say, what they mean by it, and how they spell and pronounce it. But many of us would rather stand up for *good* usage—as in, let's avoid confusing or misleading anyone who listens to or reads us, and let's try not to make well-read and well-educated people wince.

Unlike some other current dictionaries, *MWC* doesn't so much as hint that there are people to whom *compare to* means something different from *compare with*. It says nothing to warn

people off the verb phrase *impact on* or the verb *impact* in figurative uses, and it gives without comment *impactful* and *im-
pactive* as adjectives. It calls certain subjective and objective uses
of *myself* "standard"; among its examples are "others and *myself*
continued to press for the legislation" and "for my wife and *myself* it was a happy time."

There's a philosophy behind all this, of course. And people who
know their way around usage manuals and stylebooks don't necessarily consider *MWC*'s permissiveness a problem: if they want
niceties explained, they look elsewhere. But any of us who feel we
can use all the help we can get to maintain useful traditional distinctions and forms of expression will do well to remain cautious
around *MWC*.

❖

Webster's New World College Dictionary, fourth edition (1999), has
been growing on me. The official dictionary of the Associated
Press, *The New York Times,* and *The Wall Street Journal, WNW* is
current, it's diverse, it steers people toward traditional usage that
no one will consider incorrect, and it packs a lot in. For instance,
it calls *alright* a disputed spelling of *all right*—and that's everything it has to say on the subject. But for the purposes of newspaper reporters on deadline, and no doubt others who appreciate
getting a simple answer when they ask a simple question, it's
enough, no? In contrast, the *AHD* supplies a 114-word usage note:
"Despite the appearance of the form *alright* in works of such well-
known writers as Langston Hughes and James Joyce, the single
word spelling has never been accepted as standard. This is pecu-
liar, since similar fusions such as *already* and *altogether* have never
raised any objections. . . ." The *RHUD* devotes fifty-three words to

alright versus *all right*. *WNW* contains few usage notes and few visuals (only a minority of pages include pictures) but a goodly number of basic synonymies.

As for the CD-ROM, I find it perfectly serviceable, but there's no use in my going on about it, because between the day I shipped this book's manuscript off to the publisher and when the printed book arrived in bookstores, a new edition of the *WNW* CD-ROM was released. I would guess that the new one is better than ever.

❖

As I've said, *The American Heritage Dictionary* is the resource to which I usually turn first. I've relied on it for decades, so I know it well. Nowadays, I'm proud to say, I'm even a member of its usage panel. To the extent that all this amounts to an implied recommendation, I suppose I'd better tell you what I don't like about the *AHD* as well as what I do.

What I like: The current, fourth edition (published in 2000) is by far the handsomest dictionary out there, with well-planned illustrations, diagrams, maps, and photographs on nearly every page, in color throughout.

The *AHD* is strong on diversity without hammering you over the head with its righteousness. For instance, here's how it defines *girl:*

1. A female child.
2. An immature or inexperienced woman, especially a young woman.
3. A daughter: *our youngest girl.*
4. *Informal.* A grown woman: *a night out with the girls.*
5. A female who comes from or belongs to a particular place: *a city girl.*
6. *Offensive.* A female servant, such as a maid.
7. A female sweetheart: *cadets escorting their girls to the ball.*

And that just about covers it, I think, though I would have liked to see a little warning attached to meaning 4, to the effect that men striving for an informal tone with women they don't know well had better steer clear.

The *AHD* contains so many usage notes and other worthy asides that it can do double duty as a usage manual, or maybe even a primer on linguistics. For instance, here's part of an "Our Living Language" note, on the subject of the "invariant *be*":

In place of the inflected forms of *be*, such as *is* and *are*, used in Standard English, African American Vernacular English (AAVE) and some varieties of Southern American English may use zero copula or an invariant *be*, as in *He be working*, instead of the Standard English *He is usually working*. As an identifying feature of the vernacular of many African Americans, invariant *be* in recent years has been frequently seized on by writers and commentators trying to imitate or parody Black speech. However, most imitators use it simply as a substitute for *is*, as in *John be sitting in that chair now*, without realizing that within AAVE, invariant *be* is used primarily for habitual or extended actions set in the present. . . .

I didn't know that.

Among the aspects of the *AHD* that I'm less fond of is that by my count it contains fewer up-to-the-minute coinages than its competitors. Its etymologies are rudimentary (no worse than average, I'd say, but no better), and it doesn't give even rough dates of the first appearances of words in print.

More important, its editors have slowly been whittling away at its standing as the most prescriptive of America's dictionaries. The first edition was published in 1969, in response to what many saw as an abdication of responsibility by Merriam-Webster eight years earlier, when that company supplanted the magisterial *Webster's Second* with the loosey-goosey *Webster's Third*.

In the first edition of the *AHD* the usage note about *hopefully* read, in its entirety:

Hopefully, as used to mean it is to be hoped or let us hope, is still not accepted by a substantial number of authorities on grammar and usage. The following example of *hopefully* in this sense is acceptable to only 44 per cent of the Usage Panel: *Hopefully, we shall complete our work in June.*

The usage note in the current edition runs to 307 words, of which here I've reproduced about two thirds:

Writers who use *hopefully* as a sentence adverb, as in *Hopefully the measures will be adopted,* should be aware that the usage is unacceptable to many critics, including a large majority of the Usage Panel. It is not easy to explain why critics dislike this use of *hopefully.* The use is justified by analogy to similar uses of many other adverbs, as in *Mercifully, the play was brief* or *Frankly, I have no use for your friend.* And though this use of *hopefully* may have been a vogue word when it first gained currency back in the early 1960s, it has long since lost any hint of jargon or pretentiousness for the general reader. The wide acceptance of the usage reflects popular recognition of its usefulness; there is no precise substitute. . . . In the 1969 Usage Panel survey, 44 percent of the Panel approved the usage, but this dropped to 27 percent in our 1986 survey. (By contrast, 60 percent in the latter survey accepted the comparable use of *mercifully* in the sentence *Mercifully, the game ended before the opponents could add another touchdown to the lopsided score.*) It is not the use of sentence adverbs per se that bothers the Panel; rather, the specific use of *hopefully* in this way has become a shibboleth.

So while a growing majority of the "people with a critical interest in the language" who make up the panel objects to the "let's hope" use of *hopefully*, the usage note has also been growing, in order to editorialize against the strictures that the members of the panel are in favor of. I don't understand this. And it's not an isolated case. Under *myself*, the first edition of the *AHD* simply reported that an overwhelming majority of the usage panel disapproved of using the word as a subject or an object of a sentence. Under *unique*, it warned against modifying this adjective (with, say, *rather* or *the most*) and left it at that. But now the usage note at *myself* reads, in part: "Although these usages have been common in the writing of reputable authors for several centuries. . . . [a] large majority of the Usage Panel disapproves. . . ." And *unique*: "Most of the Usage Panel supports this traditional view. Eighty percent disapprove of the sentence *Her designs are quite unique in today's fashions*. But. . . . *unique* appears as a modified adjective in the work of many reputable writers." Harumph.

Also unfortunately, the technological abilities of the *American Heritage* on CD-ROM took a nosedive around the turn of the century, when Microsoft stopped buying the rights to include the *AHD* in the Microsoft Bookshelf CD-ROM and brought out its own Encarta Reference sets. The electronic *AHD* has yet to recover fully. Its CD-ROM cross-referencing and searching abilities are basic—this is the only dictionary that won't whisk you off to the entry for a word when you click on it in a definition or an example. Only a tiny minority of the visuals in the print edition are reproduced onscreen. And I would never have figured out from the instructions that the CD-ROM's contents could be installed on my computer's hard drive (thereby making the computerized dictionary work much faster and freeing up the CD-ROM drive). Instead, I learned this from a reader review someone wrote on Amazon.com to help previous reviewers who were similarly flummoxed.

The *AHD* isn't the house dictionary of any huge or especially influential organizations I'm aware of. Nonetheless, several well-placed people in journalism and publishing have told me that the *AHD* is their favorite dictionary too. If you'd like to get to know the *AHD* better before you decide whether to buy a copy—or if you're a Mac user, unable to get the *AHD* on CD-ROM—you'll find the *AHD*'s entries accessible from a number of Web sites, including www.bartleby.com, www.dictionary.com, and www.yourdictionary.com.

❖

Perhaps one or another of these dictionaries is already whispering seductively in your ear. If not, here's how to narrow down the list of ones you might like. Presumably you want the dictionary in order to answer language questions that come up from time to time, yes? So make a note of each of the next half dozen or so questions that arise, and then take your list of questions to the largest brick-and-mortar bookstore you can get to conveniently. At one bookstore in my town, I found just three of the seven dictionaries. Another down the street—a chain bookstore—had six: not bad. All copies of three of them were shrink-wrapped, but when I asked a clerk if I might open them to take a look, she said, Certainly. Help yourself!

If you can't find a bookstore with a good selection of dictionaries, try the biggest library available to you. The library probably won't have the latest edition of each dictionary, but never mind. Dramatic makeovers from one edition to the next are almost unknown; only your questions about new words and usages will go unanswered. Now look your questions up. See which dictionary or dictionaries answer them in a way that satisfies you. Flip through the contenders you like so far and see what combination of attributes ultimately pleases you the most. If you're a computer user and you're at a bookstore, be sure at least to consider buying an edition that comes with a CD-ROM; if you're at the library, go home and hunt up that version from an online store. Sometimes the book-plus-CD-ROM editions can be annoying to find online, because they're a hybrid product—but persevere.

Here's a little out-of-nowhere tip for bons vivants: curling up with a nice hot cup of cocoa or tea or even a martini can transform reading a new dictionary's front matter from a chore into a rarefied pleasure.

A person who has decided on a dictionary and has at least begun to get acquainted with it is ready to branch out beyond the dictionary, in order to answer other kinds of language questions, including some that lexicographers can only dream of.

CHAPTER FOUR

The Infinite Resource

This is the geeky chapter, but the material in it is crucial, and not all of it is dull.

> "Is there a word for 'killing your husband'? Some equivalent to *parricide, fratricide, uxoricide*? I can't seem to think of it."

The reason my correspondent was asking was none of my business. I e-mailed him right back:

> Why, that would be *mariticide*!

People often send me language questions that have been bothering them for hours, days, even years. When I shoot them an answer right back (sorry, I don't always—just when I have time), they're flabbergasted.

A few minutes later this arrived:

> "Did you already know the word *mariticide*? If so, whoa! If not, I'm curious how you found it."

I realized a long time ago that I don't have to know much of anything so long as I'm good at looking things up. Because you already had the Latin *-icide* ending, your question boiled down to,
What's the Latin for *husband*? So I called up a search engine
and typed in *"husband in Latin."* The list of results that came
back consisted mainly of sites on which Latinas were seeking
proposals of marriage. But I also found a Latin-English dictionary and a "Word of the Day" page on a site called Travlang
(www.travlang.com), which each day translates a word into
eighty-some languages. One day's word was *husband,* and the
Latin was said to be *maritus.* (If your computer has speakers,
you can even click on the translations and hear them aloud.
Want to hear how the word for *husband* is pronounced in Latin—
or Latvian or Luganda? Just click.) Having found the Latin word,
I simply replaced its ending with *-icide* and verified the result in
my *Webster's Third.* Voilà!

Alternatively, I suppose, I could have found *mariticide* by
searching the *Webster's Third* CD-ROM for **icide.* But that wild-
card search yields 113 entries, and I would have had to review the
unfamiliar ones (*acaricide*? *ascaricide*?) individually. The Internet
method was a lot faster. Since that e-mail exchange, I've come
across several more Web sites that include Latin-English dictionaries. And out in the real world I happened on and bought a secondhand Latin-English dictionary, which gives *maritus.* Not everyone
wants to be surrounded by reference books, though, especially now
that the Internet is handy.

I've already mentioned a few specific dictionary Web sites, but
those amount to a new format for information that already was or
could have been available to us, in books or on CD-ROMs. The In-

ternet also offers us information that was never before available, or that we would have had to go to a great deal of trouble to get— mountains, avalanches, landslides, deluges, torrents, tsunamis, of information. Sometimes the Internet straightforwardly presents us with answers to our questions. These may come from authoritative sources or quacks or anything in between; further along we'll consider how to tell the difference (it's not always easy). And sometimes the Internet lets us tease out what we want to know from material intended to tell us something else.

By "tease out" I mean, for instance, that Amazon.com and other online booksellers post information about books in order to make it simple and appealing for us to buy them—but maybe you'd just like to see whether a particular book is in print and confirm that in something you're writing you have the title correctly rendered and the author's name correctly spelled. (If so, bless you.) When looking into something like this, you'll do fine using the Internet as long as you proceed cautiously. I say "cautiously" because, for instance, the images of a book's covers and interior pages on online booksellers' sites are more reliable than the site's own text. Even the images are not foolproof, however, because book covers, and titles, can change.

What's more, the publication dates you'll find are definitely not trustworthy. For recent books, online booksellers tend to tell you when they began (or will begin) selling them, not the official publication date, which may be different by a month or more. So a book that a site says was published in November or December of one year might, for the record, have been published the year after. And for older books, the sites are likely to tell you the year when the edition they're selling was issued, not when the first edition was published. It's best to get the basic information, including the name of the publisher, from the online bookseller, and if for any reason this is suspect, check your facts on the publisher's, a library's, or another Web site. Yes, double-checking is more trouble than just reproducing the first thing you see—but it's less trouble than getting accurate information tended to be in the pre-Internet era, and it's less embarrassing than goofing everything up.

Discussing the Internet as a language resource might until recently have been perceived as elitist: not everyone has a computer and a high-speed Internet connection, I know. But nowadays most public libraries offer Internet access. In fact, why don't we take that assertion as a little case study: how can I possibly know that with any certainty? Well, if I look up *public libraries* and *Internet* on an Internet news database—in this case, Google News, about which more later—those words call up hundreds of recent articles from credible sources, such as the Web sites of newspapers, radio stations, and television networks. Many of the articles are reporting or opining about anti-pornography filters on library computers (a topic that, as of this writing, has recently been in the news). But there's also a syndicated column by James J. Kilpatrick that says: "Libraries. . . . still house books, of course, but for many patrons the big attraction is the computer and its access to the Internet. By 2000, [Supreme Court Chief Justice William] Rehnquist noted, 95 percent of America's public libraries provided such access." I'll believe that.

The media is ordinarily a secondary source, reporting what goes on elsewhere—as that Kilpatrick column does. But it's a primary source when you want to know, as I often do, about journalists' use of language. News databases let us treat broad swaths of media as a primary source. Before we get into that aspect of using the Internet, though, let's look into what we can learn from Internet sources of other kinds, including what most people would think of as primary sources imparting firsthand information. To get at this material, a tool you simply can't do without is a search engine—or better yet, since you can use the great majority of search engines free, two or three.

Straight From the Source

There's little point in my giving you a detailed account of the strengths and weaknesses of particular search engines, because like everything else on the Internet, the search engines keep changing. All the same, I hope the site called Search Engine Watch (at searchenginewatch.com—that's right, there's no "www," though I'll include one in any Internet address that does start that way) sticks around and remains true to its purpose for a good long time. It is a terrific source of objective, up-to-date information on the search engines available, both all-purpose and specialized ones. Have a look at its "Web Searching Tips" and "Search Engine Listings" for a crash course in search-enginology. Or talk to your well-wired friends. I can't possibly explain as thoroughly as you deserve how search engines work and how best to use them.

The various engines perform their searches in different ways and are even more distinctly different than the various dictionaries. I know people who swear by All the Web, AltaVista, Ask Jeeves, Teoma, and Yahoo, among others, and connoisseurs use different engines to answer different kinds of questions. Google (www .google.com) is now the Internet's most widely used search engine, and it is the one I generally turn to first.

Much as it's necessary to read the front matter of a dictionary in order to interpret what the book as a whole is telling you, it's necessary to read the search engine's instructions about how to search efficiently and accurately. On Google's "Search Help" pages, for instance, you'll learn that if you want Google to search for an exact phrase, you should put quotation marks around it when you type it into the search window. You'll also learn that Google is not "case sensitive": as far as it's concerned, *Search Engines, search engines,* SEARCH ENGINES, and *sEaRcH eNgInEs* are all the same. The one exception is the word OR, which, with both letters in uppercase, amounts to a request to search for Web pages containing either of two terms. If you type in *search* OR *engines,* for example, Google will fetch pages that contain either word. And it disregards punctuation, so a search for *engines* will also yield pages containing *engine's* and *engines'*. The foregoing is true—for Google—as of this writing, but, again, things change. Read your "Search Help."

"Isn't it true that Harry S Truman had only a middle initial and not a middle name, so it's incorrect to put a period after the *S?*"

When I searched for *"harry s truman,"* right at the top of the list of responses that Google returned was the official Web site for the Truman Presidential Museum and Library, whose Internet address is www.trumanlibrary.org. On a "Truman Trivia" page on the site, the following appears: "What was Truman's middle name? Should there be a period after the S?" And the answer:

. . . The evidence provided by Mr. Truman's own practice argues strongly for the use of the period. While, as many people do, Mr. Truman often ran the letters in his signature together in a single stroke, the archives of the Harry S. Truman Library has [*sic*] numerous examples of the signature written at various times throughout Mr. Truman's lifetime where his use of a period after the "S" is very obvious.

Mr. Truman apparently initiated the "period" controversy in 1962 when, perhaps in jest, he told newspapermen that the period should be omitted. In explanation he said that the "S" did not stand for any name but was a compromise between the names of his grandfathers, Anderson Shipp Truman and Solomon Young.

Several widely recognized style manuals provide guidance in favor of using the period. . . . Most published works using the name Harry S. Truman employ the period. . . . Authoritative publications produced by the Government Printing Office consistently use the period in Mr. Truman's name. . . .

If you like, the page itself will show and tell you more, even reproducing an example of Truman's signature with a prominent period. But here you have the answer to your question.

"An editor I work with wants to change *Alaska Natives* to *Alaskan Native Americans,* since it's not obvious that *Alaska Native* is understood properly (at least outside Alaska) to refer to Native Americans living in that state. What are your thoughts?"

According to Google searches I conducted for you, "about 558,000" Web pages contain the phrase *Alaska Native,* whereas only about 1,850—a third of one percent as many—contain *Alaskan Native American.* Furthermore, skimming the snippets of text in the lists that the search engine generated, I found that many of the *Alaskan Native American* references were in fact the first three words of *Alaskan Native / American Indian* or *Alaskan Native, American Indian* or the like. (Again, Google ignores punctuation.) Web pages from the U.S. Census Bureau, the U.S. Department of Justice, and the Environmental Protection Agency all use the phrase *Alaska Native*. It seems to me you should feel free to do so too.

The *AHD*, alone among our seven dictionaries, gives an entry for *Alaska Native*, and it also discusses the term briefly in a usage note at *Native American*. These mentions should reassure us that *Alaska Native* is a bona fide term. But when you're trying to decide whether a term is "understood properly," that's something else again. In the *AHD*, not far from the *Alaska Native* entry is one for *alastor*, for example—and if you wonder whether people are likely to understand that word, you might try typing it into a search-engine window. You'll probably find, as I did, a poem with that title by Percy Bysshe Shelley, some pages for a despondent-looking eponymous rock band, stuff like that. And you'll probably conclude that if you want to use *alastor*, most people won't understand it properly unless you explain it. According to the *AHD*, an alastor is "an avenging deity or spirit, the masculine personification of Nemesis, frequently evoked in Greek tragedy." Why *doesn't* that come up more often in everyday conversation?

"Help! One space or two between full sentences?"

Type *"one space or two"* into a search-engine window and you'll find various answers to this question, including this from the *Chicago Manual of Style* Q&A page:

Q. . . . I have confusion regarding the correct spacing after periods and other closing punctuation. . . . Everything I read in manuals and from technical writers directs me to use one space after periods. I find that it works very well, except occasionally, when an extra space helps readability. . . . Others are unpleased with the one space, they think they have difficulty reading. . . . What do you think?

A. The view at CMS is that there is no reason for two spaces after a period in published work. Some people, however—my colleagues included—prefer it, relegating this preference to their personal correspondence and notes. I've noticed in old American books printed in the few decades before and after the turn of the last century (ca. 1870–1930 at least) that there seemed to be a trend in publishing to use extra space (sometimes quite a bit of it) after periods. And many people were taught to use that extra space in typing class (I was). But introducing two spaces after the period causes problems. . . .

So there.

Over the years I've read a lot of portentous stuff about how skeptical we all need to be when using the Internet and what a lot of misinformation is lurking there. To be honest, I thought I knew how to tell an authoritative source from a benighted one until, for *The Atlantic*'s Word Court, I trusted a Web site more than I should have. The question I'd been asked seemed straightforward enough, and I was satisfied that I'd answered it.

"Certain holidays upset me because I find myself bombarded by grammatically incorrect advertisements. Obviously, *Veteran's Day* and *President's Day* are incorrect. But which is correct, *Veterans'* or *Veterans*? *Presidents'* or *Presidents*?"

Let's go ask the U.S. government: typing *"federal holidays"* into the Google window ought to take us where we want to be. When the list of responses comes back, don't just pay attention to the first, headlinish line but also look at the Internet addresses, or URLs (the initials stand for "uniform [or 'universal'] resource locator"), which are generally the last or nearly the last line of each entry.

Here's www.opm.gov/fedhol—that seems promising. Sure enough, it's the site for the federal Office of Personnel Management, and it spells the holidays *Veterans Day* and . . . *Washington's Birthday*??

A note at the bottom of the page reads:

"Washington's Birthday" is the designated holiday in section 6103(a) of title 5 of the United States Code, which is the law that specifies holidays for Federal employees. Though other institutions such as state and local governments and private businesses may use other names, it is our policy to always refer to holidays by the names designated in the law.

What's *that* about? To find out, let's type *"washingtons birthday"* and *"presidents day"*—with quotation marks around each phrase but, again, never mind about apostrophes or caps—into Google, and see what we get. From the Embassy of the United States of America in Stockholm:

Until 1971, both February 12 and February 22 were observed as federal holidays to honor the birthdays of Abraham Lincoln (Feb. 12) and George Washington (Feb. 22).

In 1971 President Richard Nixon proclaimed one single federal holiday, the *Presidents' Day*, to be observed on the third Monday of February, honoring all past presidents of the United States of America.

Please Note: The Federal statute designates this day as Washington's Birthday, President Nixon issued a proclamation declaring the holiday as "Presidents' Day" in 1971. President Nixon erroneously believed that a Presidential proclamation on the matter carried the same weight as an Executive Order.

Since that change in 1971, the common term has been "Presidents' Day".

On the matter of *Washington* versus *President* in the name of the holiday, that seems credible—but are we sure we believe the site about where the apostrophe goes? Note that whoever wrote that text has used a comma splice in the first sentence after "Please Note" and put the period at the very end outside the quotation marks. Neither of these is standard practice—at least, in American English, the form of the language we'd expect from a U.S. government Web site. Typos and grammatical errors are red flags: full professional attention has not been paid.

So let's search for *"presidents day"* alone and find a more nearly definitive source. Granted, we've just learned that it's *states'* prerogative to call the holiday by this name, so you might want to look up your own state's calendar of holidays. But if we're looking for one answer for the whole country, how about www.whitehouse.gov/history/presidents? That page, under the heading "Events & Traditions," has a listing for *Presidents' Day.*

Veterans Day and *Presidents' Day,* then, appear to be the way to go—and let's just not worry that they're inconsistent with each other.

But before a condensed version of that answer was published, Joshua Friedman, a member of the magazine's fact-checking staff, did some more Internet searching—even unto the archives of the Richard Nixon Library and Birthplace. What he found proved that the part of this tale that's about Nixon is a canard. (When you think about it, why *would* the U.S. Embassy in Stockholm be the last word on *Presidents' Day* versus *Washington's Birthday*?) The reason the holiday's official federal name is Washington's Birthday, though everyone calls it Presidents' Day, turned out to be so obscure that we couldn't pin it down on the Internet. Even a phone call to the journalist I cited in the reply as it was printed couldn't clarify things completely. Ultimately, we ran with as much as we knew to be true, replacing the material from and relating to the embassy with:

> What's *that* about? Some say President Richard Nixon thought he had renamed the holiday but inadvertently failed to make the change official. Often cited as evidence is a piece in the *Arkansas Democrat-Gazette,* in which Nixon explains he wanted to honor all Presidents, "even myself"—but its author, Michael Storey, is a humor columnist, not an investigative reporter. Regardless, the common term is now *Presidents' Day,* and even the White House uses it.

Cautiously, cautiously . . . It's clear to me that my Internet connection offers me a great deal more authoritative information, much more readily, than anything else in my house or office. And yet it is easy—as we've just seen—to get things wrong if you use the Internet incautiously. The problem is not just that people and organizations with Web pages don't always know what they're talking about. Most Web sites are not proofread to a professional standard, and this is important to keep in mind when you're studying words, spellings, idioms, and punctuation. Furthermore, most of what looks like research online is being done by machines—the search engines—which are incapable of thinking; they are simply turning up data that may (or may not) help you find out what you want to know. You have to think for them.

But as we've also just seen, there's no ineffable mystery to picking definitive sources out of the crowd. I mean, if you want solid information about the health benefits of ginkgo biloba, would you choose to read an article from *Scientific American* and one written by the director of drug therapy management and the chair of the Human Research Committee at the Massachusetts General Hospital (I easily found both of these articles online), or would you turn to www.sea-energy.biz or dreampharm.com? It's also important to pay attention to the date a page was written or posted on the Internet. Obviously, a five-year-old article about ginkgo biloba, even if it is from a source you'd trust if you saw the article in print, won't give you current information.

These principles apply to researching all kinds of questions, including ones about words. I don't mean to say that the Internet contains a definitive answer to every word question. Again as with dictionaries, a lack of response or at least of informed consensus is implicitly an answer too.

> "I was told the longest word in the English language in 1939 was *pneumonoultramicroscopicsilicovulcanoconeosis* (an inflammation of the linings of the lungs caused by the inhalation of minute particles of silicon, i.e. coal dust; it's 'black lung'). But where do I get a list of the longest words in the English language for every other year?"

Now, that's a strange question. Does the man who asked it think that each year brings us a new, longer word? Or does he think that someone somewhere keeps track of the longest word to appear in print in any given year? Never mind. Let's see if we can find out something more or less relevant to tell him.

I copied *pneumonoultramicroscopicsilicovulcanoconeosis* into Google's window and the news that came back was that this word "did not match any documents." But, Google asked, did I mean *pneumonoultramicroscopicsilicovolcanoconiosis*? (I love it when Google does that. The reason it asks, of course, is not that someone behind the scenes has thought up all the spelling mistakes users might make and helpfully corrected them in advance. Rather, citations are available to Google for the respelling it suggests.) And, sure enough, that does seem to be what I, or you, meant. "About 1,890" sites included the latter word.

Unfortunately, none of the top fifty seemed prepared to answer anything like your question—though I did read that our word actually dates back to 1935, when evidently it appeared (with a *k* rather than a *c* following the *volcano* part) in the *New York Herald-Tribune*. Several sites quoted (accurately) the *Oxford English Dictionary*, which calls *pneumonoultramicroscopicsilicovolcanoconiosis* (*-koniosis*) "a factitious word alleged to mean 'a lung disease caused by the inhalation of very fine silica dust' but occurring chiefly as an instance of a very long word."

I also searched for *"longest words"* and got a range of intriguing if suspect information. One site showed me a word of 1,909 letters that it said is the "scientific name for Trypthophan synthetase," a protein containing 267 amino acids. When I searched for *"trypthophan synthetase,"* though, Google asked me whether I meant *tryptophan synthetase,* which matched about 8,750 pages, as opposed to *trypthophan*'s six. The site with the 1,909-letter word stated that "deoxyribonucleic acid (DNA) is alleged to have 207,000 letters, but has never been printed in full." OK, now we can be sure we're dealing with someone who is in over his or her head, inasmuch as the English-language name of DNA is, obviously, *deoxyribonucleic acid*—a term that contains twenty letters. Scientists use A, C, G, and T to designate the four "chemical building blocks" that make up all of DNA—so in this sense DNA "has" letters. But human DNA is about three billion of those letters long, or so I am told by the Web site for the Human Genome Project, which recently finished cataloguing "about 99 percent of the human genome's gene-containing regions . . . sequenced to an accuracy of 99.99 percent."

Another "longest words" site presented the coinage *Bababadalgharaghtakamminapronnkonnbronntonnepronntuonnthunntrovarrhounawnskawntoohoohoordeenenthurnuk,* explaining (and simultaneously undercutting its authority by misspelling *page* and *Finnegans*): "This word is on the first pate of Finegans Wake by James Joyce, and is a symbolic thunderclap representing the fall of Adam and Eve." The Web page says that Joyce's word contains 100 letters, though its rendering of the word has 101. And there are three typos in that rendering, all extra letters: what Joyce wrote was just 98 letters long. (How do I know that? Easy—I found page one of the printed book on Amazon.com, and compared it.) But at least *bababadal. . .* is a word to which we can assign a year: 1939, when *Finnegans Wake* was published. (And how do I know that? From Amazon cross-checked with a James Joyce biography site.) The very longest word known to the creator of the *bababadal. . .* site contains 3,600 letters and is a "chemical name describing bovine NADP–specific glutamate dehydrogenase, which contains 500 amino acids"—here we go again.

I warned you we probably weren't going to be able to answer that person's question. But we found out more than I thought we might.

❖

"We all know the meaning of the expression *silver lining* or the saying *When in Rome, do as the Romans do*. But what about the expression *a moose on the table*? Have you heard it before? The expression *a moose on the table* was recently introduced to indicate a discussion about a difficult and unpleasant subject. Is there a synonym for *a moose on the table*?"

I would hardly know where to start looking into this if it weren't for the Internet.

A businessman named Randall Tobias coined the phrase, which now seems to have spread throughout management circles. Do you remember when, in May of 2003, *The New York Times* was in turmoil and held a town-meeting-style event for its newsroom staff? And, to the journalists' consternation, the publisher, Arthur Sulzberger Jr., who was onstage, produced a stuffed toy moose? If not, you can read up on the incident by searching for *"arthur sulzberger" "toy moose."*

According to the *Indy Men's Magazine* site (all right, all right, it isn't Holy Scripture, but it does quote the man who coined the phrase):

When Randall Tobias took over as the Chairman and CEO of Eli Lilly and Company in the early 1990s, he . . . noticed that Lilly's culture had a palpable flaw: Employees were occasionally reluctant to speak their minds in the presence of senior leaders.

"We've all been in meetings where there's an issue before the group that everyone recognizes is hanging out there," says Tobias, "but no one wants to be the first to acknowledge. I have always thought of such issues as being like a large moose on the middle of the proverbial meeting table—it's sort of hard to ignore, but everyone pretends it just isn't there. 'Let's get the moose on the table' was a colorful way of saying, 'let's not be afraid to express opinions openly and honestly.'"

Now, by the way, Tobias, with his son Todd Tobias, has written a book titled *Put the Moose on the Table: Lessons in Leadership From a CEO's Journey Through Business and Life.*

❖

You just never know what the Internet is going to be able to answer credibly until you try.

"*Appaloosa Journal* is a horse magazine, and sometimes we write about horses destroyed by euthanasia. We've used *euthanize* as the verb form, but the American Veterinary Medical Association uses *euthanatize*. What's correct?"

Because I have heard *euthanatize* rarely if ever, your e-mail made me wonder what the American Veterinary Medical Association is up to. I found its position succinctly explained in a 1996 issue of "Lab Animal Line," published by the Office of the University Veterinarian of the University of Kentucky:

Euthanasia is a composite of two Greek word forms: "eu" meaning well, good, or easy, and "thanatos" meaning death. Dr. W. A. Aitken, former Editor-in-Chief (1952–1959) of the *Journal of the American Veterinary Medical Association* (*JAVMA*), after consulting with a language scholar, concluded that, in the verb form, as much of the root expression (thanatos) should be retained as possible in words of Greek origin. The verb form "euthanatize" is listed as a first choice in Merriam-Webster's Collegiate Dictionary, Electronic Version. . . . We should all strive to be "on the same page" and use "euthanatize" in our daily speech and our protocol applications.

Neither online nor in print, however, does *Merriam-Webster's Collegiate* continue to prefer *euthanatize,* nor does any other American dictionary I know of except creaky old *Webster's Third.* And searches in two news databases brought up, respectively, 156 recent citations for *euthanize* but none for *euthanatize,* and 91 for *euthanize* but none for *euthanatize.* It's presumptuous of me to be telling the American Veterinary Medical Association its business, but the page the rest of us are on now is *euthanize.*

A similarly abstruse but more entertaining bit of language information that I needed the Internet to track down is a joke involving a duck and Chapstick. A few years ago William Whitworth, when he was *The Atlantic*'s editor in chief, read the galleys of an article I was editing about an ornithological expedition. The author had included the duck joke in question for comic relief, but when Bill got to it, he realized he'd heard it before. One of the many plagiarism scandals that have erupted in the past few years had just broken, and Bill asked me to get rid of the joke, because it wasn't original and there was no telling where it was from.

The author, however, balked. She liked the joke. I typed *duck* and *chapstick* into a search engine and immediately discovered a wide world of duck-joke Web sites listing her joke. Nowhere did I find it attributed to any particular author, but often humor that does have an author isn't attributed; it just circulates and recirculates, and no one bothers to give credit where credit is due. The argument that at last persuaded the author to cut the joke, though, was that clearly it had been around for a while—so long that it even has a naughty variant, also readily findable online (search for *duck chapstick condom*). And if Bill Whitworth—not a man to whom many of us would be inclined to tell a duck joke—had heard it, surely so had lots of the magazine's readers. If you don't know the joke, give the search-engine method a try. You'll also find a joke about a duck that keeps asking someone for grapes (or corn), which is pretty funny too.

❖

"Supposedly there are three words in the English language ending in *-gry*. *Angry* and *hungry* are two of them. What is the third?"

So I typed *angry hungry words* into my search window. Among the responses I got was this, among the "Frequently Asked Questions" on Dictionary.com:

Q. Besides angry and hungry, is there another common English word that ends in -gry?

A. No. . . . [T]he question comes up so frequently . . . because of a riddle. One version of the riddle goes, "Think of words ending in -GRY. Angry and hungry are two of them. There are only three words in the English language. What is the third word? The word is something that everyone uses every day. If you have listened carefully, I have already told you what it is."

The answer is "language," because "language" is the third word in the phrase "the English language." Two of the sentences thus have absolutely nothing to do with the question: "Think of words ending in -GRY. Angry and hungry are two of them." They are there only to throw you off course. What's left is the actual riddle itself: "There are only three words in the English language. What is the third word? The word is something that everyone uses every day. If you have listened carefully, I have already told you what it is." . . .

But that might not be the answer; that might not even be the question. In his remarkable book *Wordplay*, Chris Cole gives a historical account of the riddle and seven different versions of it with seven different answers. . . .

Yahoo even has a category devoted to it, if you still haven't had enough of this most maddening riddle.

Virtual Libraries

Another invaluable Internet resource is what I call libraries. Some of the best of these consist of links, maintained by a person or an organization with a reason to keep them up to date, to numerous useful and authoritative sources. Others contain the text of reference books or classic literature right on the site.

Are you a fan of *The New York Times*? Then maybe you'd like to get to know Navigator, "the home page used by the newsroom of *The New York Times* for forays into the Web." The page states that "its primary intent is to give reporters and editors new to the Web a solid starting point for a wide range of journalistic functions without forcing all of them to spend time wandering around blindly to find a useful set of links of their own." When I last looked, the Navigator home page was a portal to nearly three hundred sites as various as Roget's Internet Thesaurus, National Geographic's Map Machine, and the Urban Legends Reference Pages. Navigator's Web address is www.nytimes.com/navigator.

The New York Public Library, at www.nypl.org, has a "Best of the Web" compendium of thousands of informative sites. The

Council of Science Editors, at www.councilscienceeditors.org, has "Reference Links"; and something called Sphinx has a wide-ranging "Reference Shelf" at www.nmia.com/~sphinx/refrence.htm. (Yes, "refrence" is correct in that URL.) Enormous searchable archives of literature and reference books, including many of special interest to language mavens, reside at www.bartleby.com, www.bibliomania.com, www.ipl.org (the abbreviation stands for "Internet Public Library"), and promo.net/pg ("pg" stands for Project Gutenberg).

Furthermore, as the proud holder of a Boston Public Library card, I wonder if maybe you, too, are a card-carrying library patron. Even as I sit at home or work, by visiting the BPL's site and typing in my card number I throw open the lid on a treasure chest of resources.

The Power of the Press

Much of the foregoing is Internet 101 stuff. The publicly available Web tool best able to revolutionize language reference in particular, however, is the news database, made up of the contents of professionally edited media—newspaper, magazine, and journal articles, transcripts from radio and television stations, and sometimes additional material from these media outlets' Web sites. Those of us who are devotees of H. W. Fowler and his masterwork, *A Dictionary of Modern English Usage,* love this book chiefly for Fowler's point of view and the way he expresses it. But Fowler is also awe-inspiring for the sheer quantity of close reading he must have done to collect citations that demonstrate grammatical and usage errors. His efforts may well remain forever unsurpassed, for news databases can now greatly simplify such hunts.

If we search the Internet as a whole not for information (as we have been doing until now) but, as Fowler might, for the language in which information is conveyed, at best we'll discover how every person, place, and thing with a Web site spells or uses a word or expression. I don't mind knowing this. But for us to review and pass judgment on the language seen on the Internet as a whole would be almost as if Fowler had collected and critiqued passages from personal letters, advertisements, and hand-lettered signs in shops, rather than from the edited media, such as newspapers, that he in fact used as sources.

What appears in edited media is an especially important level of language, for several reasons. First, it tends to have a sizable audience, so it's influential. Then, too, professional writers and editors and copy editors have generated and vetted nearly all of it, so standards of some sort are being upheld. Also, lots of conventions that are beyond the scope of dictionaries and other reference books are unselfconsciously on display here. Finally, this language is a rich lode that lexicographers mine. Words and new meanings make their way into dictionaries by, usually, appearing in print (as opposed to just coming up in private conversation) over time. So news databases can give us both information that dictionaries will never tell us and information that dictionaries haven't gotten around to sharing with us yet.

Suppose for some reason you wanted to refer to the Karakoram Highway, which runs between China and Pakistan, and sound as if you knew what you were talking about. Khunjerab Pass is a renowned scenic spot along the highway. But do its familiars say *Khunjerab Pass* or *the Khunjerab Pass*? You won't find an authoritative answer to this question in any print source I'm aware of. Nor do I know of a way to find an authoritative answer on the Internet as a whole.

Or maybe a colleague has asked you to look over a draft she has written, in which it says that something is *far afield of* something else. Wouldn't *far afield from* be more idiomatic? Can you prove that? Or maybe you've come across the word *phishing* and wonder what it means. Answers to these questions are nowhere to be found in standard dictionaries. In fact, for the purposes of this book I spent much more time trying unsuccessfully to research the *far afield* question in the reference books on my shelves than I spent answering it definitively on the Internet.

How do news databases answer these questions? Well, first let's get acquainted with the databases themselves. There are those that cost money to use, the major ones being Westlaw, Factiva, and LexisNexis. And there are those that are available free, the major one being Google News. The free AltaVista search engine has a news page as well, and this merits looking into because, at this writing, it archives articles and transcripts from more than 3,000 sources for "more than a year." In contrast, Google News keeps material from "approximately 4,500 news sources" for just a month. AltaVista's news page is newer than Google's, and I haven't yet found it to be nearly as helpful. Though it's worth keeping an eye on, I won't discuss it further here.

Bryan A. Garner, who is the editor of *Black's Law Dictionary* and the author of *Garner's Modern American Usage,* among other language-reference books, swears by Westlaw (www.westlaw.com), considering it the best database for language research. Alas, I have no experience with it, because one has to subscribe to the whole pricey package, intended for lawyers and including heaps of specialized legal-research materials, to get access to its news database, which (at this writing) is drawn from "more than 6,800 news and business publications." And when I looked into it, Westlaw's pay-as-you-go credit-card option didn't include admittance to the news database, and neither did the free two-week trial subscription that I signed up for. Factiva (www.factiva.com), which brings together "nearly 8,000 news and business information sources," also has a pay-as-you-go credit-card option. But, as I'll explain, if you're more interested in the way sources use language than in what they're using it to say, there turns out to be no way to use Factiva efficiently in terms of either money (unless you're already a subscriber) or time.

If your workplace or school gives you access to Westlaw, Factiva, or LexisNexis (www.lexisnexis.com, which we'll get to shortly) under a bulk-pricing deal, do give it a try. If not, you may want to check back with the Web sites every now and then in case their pricing has changed in your favor. Currently the most affordable option for people whose language-research needs are critical is LexisNexis's day pass or week pass.

Or you could head for Google News (news.google.com). You can't beat the price: again, it's free. What LexisNexis offers that Google News doesn't—nor does Google have plans to offer it, a company spokesperson told me—is decades' worth of archives. Nexis (which is, roughly speaking, the news component of Lexis-Nexis; Lexis is the legal database) contains nearly the full text of, for instance, *The New York Times* from June of 1980 to the present, and Associated Press stories filed since January of 1977. Few of Nexis's 14,000 sources go back so far, but still. Its archives are vast compared with the Google News rolling archive of thirty days' worth of material.

So Nexis can show you, for example, when *phishing* began to appear in print, whereas Google News shows you only how the word is being used now. Although both databases include material from all over the world, either of them will allow you to search material from American sources only—and if you're mainly interested in American English, as I am, this is a boon.

Then again, Google News can do something terrific that Nexis cannot: it can search for exact words and phrases, punctuation excepted. Common little words like *the* and *of* and *from* are beneath Nexis's notice, by design—so if you want to answer our *Khunjerab Pass* question, for instance, you'll have to search for *khunjerab pass* and then tally up which references are prefaced by *the* and which aren't.

This is easy enough to do, particularly owing to a feature that Nexis (along with Google News) has and Factiva doesn't—which is why I'm not more enthusiastic about Factiva. When asking Nexis for articles that contain *khunjerab pass,* you can request an "expanded" version of the articles it returns, in which you're shown not just what pieces from what publications contain the phrase but also every line that contains it in each piece. Factiva presents you with the list of articles but requires you to click on them one at a time and scan the text to find the language you're looking for—and if you're paying by credit card, each one of those clicks costs you money. You can ask to be shown "keywords in context" rather than the whole article, but even then you have to click on each article to see the keywords you're searching for. This works, but it can get expensive—and it takes a lot longer than just going down the list that Nexis puts in front of you. Google News, when it returns its list of results for a search, automatically shows you the word or phrase or phrases in context; you don't even have to make a special request to get it to do that.

When I used Google News to look into the *Khunjerab Pass* question, it returned just two citations, one from the *Portland* (Oregon) *Tribune* and one from the Pakistani online news service *PakTribune*. Both prefaced the phrase with *the*—but that's much too small a sample to mean anything.

When I searched Nexis for *khunjerab pass,* it called up seventy-one articles that have appeared in American newspapers and newswires since 1971. Of these, sixty-two used *the* (though four of them mentioned the pass more than once and referred to it inconsistently, at least once with *the* and once without). So only nine articles in effect voted unequivocally in favor of *Khunjerab Pass,* and I wouldn't say they came from "better" (or worse) sources than the others. It looks as if *the Khunjerab Pass* is indeed the way to go, or at least you'll have a lot more company if you say it that way.

Note, however, that if you were searching for the misspelling *Kunjerab Pass,* Nexis could easily mislead you: it presented me with six citations from U.S. newspapers and newswires, including ones from *The New York Times,* the *Chicago Tribune,* and the *Los Angeles Times,* without so much as hinting at the existence of those seventy-one *Khunjerab* citations, including ones from all three of the publications I just mentioned. But darling Google News did ask whether perchance I meant *Khunjerab* instead.

As for our other questions, when I searched Nexis for *far afield,* the database pulled up seventy U.S. newspaper and wire *far afield* citations from the previous month, of which fourteen read *far afield from* and seven read *far afield of.* (In the great majority of the others the phrase read *as far afield as* or the clause ended at *far afield.*) So *far afield from* is more common, but *far afield of* is hardly unheard of. Google News showed me just three citations for "*far afield of*" (with Google, remember to put quotation marks around the phrase or you'll get all the articles that contain both *far* and *afield,* and *of* will be ignored), and six for *"far afield from."* Here, too, the outcome was similar to Nexis's but the number of citations was so small as to make the results unreliable.

Nexis gave me forty-five American citations for *phishing* that didn't pertain to the band named Phish; most of these defined the term. For instance, from the *Chicago Tribune:* "It is an online swindle known as 'phishing,' in which computer users receive e-mails that seem to come from businesses like Paypal, Best Buy and eBay. The e-mail contains a link directing recipients to a Web site that resembles the real one. Once there, they are duped into updating billing information by entering personal and financial information." The earliest citation in Nexis of *phishing* with this meaning comes from Jacksonville's *Florida Times-Union* in March of 1997, though only lately has the term become at all common. In this case Google News showed me more citations than Nexis—fifty-three, the great majority of which defined the term pretty much the way the *Chicago Tribune* did.

So we have lots of ways to use the Internet, and these uses have implications that we'll consider further on. One implication of Internet news databases in particular is that instead of relying on, say, *The New York Times Manual of Style and Usage* or the *Associated Press Stylebook,* you can review *Times* or AP stories in the database's archives to find out what these organizations have actually published. If you like, that is, you can do as they do, not as they say. What's more, as we've seen, you can research all sorts of questions that not even the best stylebooks attempt to answer. But let's find out what stylebooks do have to offer us before deciding whether or not we need them.

CHAPTER FIVE

The Kind of Style
You Can Buy

"I am interested in unclear punctuation rules, those about which reasonable minds (and grammatical authorities) may disagree. Should I write *F.B.I.* or *FBI*? *Reenact* or *reënact*? *James'* or *James's*? Italicize *deja vu* or use diacritical marks or both?

"Right now my brother, a journalist, is writing a novel in Associated Press style, because that's what he knows. Depending on the reader's point of view, there will or will not be 'punctuation errors.' What are these quasi-errors called?

"Come to think of it, is there such a thing as a punctuationist?"

Anyone at all detail-oriented who is writing a novel, or anything else, needn't get very far into it to realize that a "house style" is going to be required. I mean, when you start your second chapter, you have to ask yourself, *Chapter Two, Chapter 2, Chapter II,* or maybe just *Two*? Well, what did you do for the first chapter? Are you happy with the way that looks?

"House style" has to do with such relatively rote matters as how to punctuate, where to use numerals and where to spell out numbers, what to capitalize or italicize, where to use symbols like *$* and *%* and where to spell the concepts out (*dollars, percent*). Some authors' minds operate on too lofty a plane for them to care about such things. Most of the professional writers I know, however, are liable to feel deeply, personally misunderstood if their editor second-guesses them about whether to capitalize the word that comes after a colon or where to use diacritical marks, such as the dieresis (on *reënact*) in the letter that begins this chapter.

When writing is going to be part of a newspaper, magazine, journal, Web site, or other medium that follows an established format, style decisions probably won't be left up to the individual writers, any more than the choice of black tie, business attire, or beachwear as appropriate dress for a party is ordinarily left to the individual guests. But when a house style isn't imposed from outside, choosing one and sticking with it will simplify your—anyone's—writing life. This applies whether your "house" is literally your house or a publishing concern or diversified multinational corporation. Certain style decisions are more compatible with other style decisions than their alternatives might be, and different constellations of decisions set different tones—as we'll see. Want to reevaluate how to set an appropriately businesslike tone every time you draft a memo at work? I didn't think so.

Ah, but let's not forget to answer my correspondent's question.

No one has yet made a career specialty out of punctuation, as far as I know, though there certainly are books about punctuation and nothing but. However, I have not found one that does a better job of communicating the rules than a good stylebook or usage manual does. "Rules" so obscure that they don't appear in the standard language-reference books aren't ones that a writer needs to worry about following. Well-known, authoritative sources give solutions to all the problems that come up often, so you (or your brother) need only choose a source and learn its rules well. If a problem is rare and you can't find a ready-made solution, go ahead and wing it. A handy principle that applies in every realm of life goes like this: The harder it is to decide which of two or more choices to make, because you can justify them equally, the less it matters which you choose.

I'd imagine that your brother's fiction has a good deal in common with his journalism, so I don't know why he shouldn't follow AP style. The *AP Stylebook*—or *Webster's New World,* the dictionary it recommends—calls for *FBI, reenact, James',* and *deja vu,* without italics. The nation's other leading stylebook, *The Chicago Manual of Style,* favors *FBI, reenact, James's,* and *déjà vu,* with the accents but again without italics.

"My wife and I live in Jerusalem, and you would think that with all the problems we have in Israel, she and I would have something more important to disagree about than punctuation. But she claims that proper usage calls for a period to come outside the quotation marks at the end of a sentence. I claim that British usage is different from American. Please save our marriage."

Punctuation conventions do indeed differ in British English and American English. British usage calls for periods, and also commas, to appear inside quotation marks when they are part of the matter quoted, but otherwise not. American usage calls for those two marks to appear inside quotation marks in all contexts, for colons and semicolons to appear outside them in pretty much all contexts, and for the placement of question marks and exclamation points to depend on meaning. In Israel today American influence predominates over British, not least because the population includes many thousands of American immigrants and their descendants. So increasingly, though not invariably, Israeli English follows U.S. conventions of punctuation.

❖

"Help! I am an editor working with an author who insists on always capitalizing *Earth*. His book is an environmental science text, so the word appears hundreds of times. For example, he says, 'Human progress often alters the *Earth*'s surface.' I have always capitalized *Earth* only when *the* does not precede it. With the use of the article, I make *earth* lowercase. Am I right? I cannot find a clear rule."

I checked half a dozen style and usage manuals for you, and I found a rule in each of them. The problem is, the rules aren't quite the same. None of the manuals, you'll be glad to know, wants to see a capital letter in the example sentence you quote. And those that mention *the* tend to agree with you that almost always when it is used, *earth* should be lowercase. However, *The New York Times Manual of Style and Usage* notes, sensibly, "The absence of *the* is not the test for capitalization, as *down to earth* and *move heaven and earth* demonstrate." In proposing what a test might be, it and several other manuals use phrases like "the proper name of the planet" and "specialized context of astronomy."

If you edit on a computer, I think (I hope!) that your search-and-replace function will come in handy as you work on this writer's book.

❖

"I had always been under the impression that when constructing a list, one should place a comma between the second-to-last element and the *and* preceding the last element of the list, and that to neglect to do so, in effect, groups the final two elements of the list as one compound element rather than two separate elements.

"Lately, however, I see more and more often (or so it seems to me) this final comma left out of lists, even in writing by those who should know better. Am I correct in assuming that the final comma is necessary?"

Over the years the phrase "those who should know better" has made me increasingly leery.

This is called a serial comma or, sometimes, an Oxford comma, and styles differ as to whether to use it. Most newspapers, including *The New York Times, The Wall Street Journal,* and papers that follow AP style, omit serial commas. The idea seems to be to put up a minimum of barriers to readers' progress. But scholarly and literary publications do typically use serial commas. *The Chicago Manual of Style,* the style bible for many such publications, "strongly recommends this widely practiced usage . . . since it prevents ambiguity." Here's an example of the ambiguity that can result: "Habitually omitting serial commas leads to inconsistency, sows confusion in readers' minds and heads their thoughts in the wrong direction."

The truth is that only rarely will the omission of a serial comma confuse anyone, even momentarily. But people who believe in serial commas—count me among them—would rather not have to scrutinize every sentence with a series in it for potential ambiguity in order to decide whether to add a comma.

I've never seen a series that was more ambiguous with a serial comma than without one.

One style or the other is usual in certain contexts, I mean to say, but both styles are in respectable use.

Relatively Speaking

About an astonishing range of things, I submit, we would all be better informed if we'd been taught not merely answers to questions but also that those are *our* answers and other valid ones are possible. This is different from situations in which there is definitely a right answer and we just don't know it—or don't know it yet. (Did Shakespeare write Shakespeare? What happened to Jimmy Hoffa?) Rather, I mean questions like St. John's wort, Prozac, or psychotherapy? Stand or draw on sixteen? To brine or not to brine a roasting chicken? Whose God is the real God?

Much of what's in stylebooks falls into this category. In, for instance, "the Tombigbee and Mobile rivers" should the *r* in the word *rivers* be capitalized? Should foreign-language titles in English contexts be capped as they would be if the words were English—say, *A la Recherche du Temps Perdu*? Or should the title be capped as it would be in the context of its own language—*A la recherche du temps perdu*? An additional twist in this example is that the initial word would take an accent grave if it were lowercase (*à*), but both English and French styles often call for accents to be left off capital letters—so should that title begin *A la* or *À la*? Or should the title be translated—and if so, literally (*In Search of Lost Time*) or according to established convention, if such a convention exists (*Remembrance of Things Past*)? Furthermore, the title we've just been obsessing about is not actually that of a book but of a *series* of books, which some styles treat differently. Maybe questions like this make your eyes glaze over—in which case, you're a trouper for having read this much of this chapter, and please feel free to move on to the next. But if you do sometimes find yourself wondering about things of this sort, you'll want to know about stylebooks.

The fundamental purpose of stylebooks is to codify how we—whoever "we" are—do things. The Modern Language Association, for example, has its *MLA Style Manual;* the American Medical Association has its *Manual of Style;* the American Psychological Association has its *Publication Manual;* the Council of Science Editors has its *Scientific Style and Format.* In other realms there are the *Associated Press Stylebook, The Chicago Manual of Style, The Gregg Reference Manual, The New York Times Manual of Style and Usage, The Wall Street Journal Guide to Business Style and Usage, Wired Style, Words into Type,* and many other stylebooks.

In this chapter I am purposely ignoring the extent to which stylebooks and usage manuals overlap. Overlap they surely do. Usage decisions are the likes of where to use *among* and where *between,* whether *It's me* is so incontrovertibly idiomatic that changing it to *It is I* would be ludicrous—and if so, is that the case in every context? Stylebooks often cover such questions, but we'll discuss that in the next chapter. And usage manuals tend to weigh in on many style questions. If you like *Garner's Modern American Usage,* for instance, you just might be able to make it your stylebook. But style questions aren't any usage manual's focus, and the manuals won't cover them as comprehensively as a good stylebook will.

Obviously, if you're a member of the MLA writing a paper you hope to publish in *PMLA* or if you're a reporter for an Associated Press newspaper, you know who you are and what style to follow, and you don't need my help, or at least you don't need much of it here.

The rest of us, though—honestly? Questions like whether to cap *rivers* in "the Tombigbee and Mobile rivers" and how to cope with *Remembrance of Things Past* aren't *that* interesting. In writing, one wants to be consistent, if only to demonstrate that one is paying attention. Furthermore, the sort of attentiveness necessary to ensure that one hasn't written "the . . . rivers" someplace and "the . . . Rivers" a few paragraphs later isn't very different from the attentiveness a person brings to bear on writing to ensure that the content isn't silly nonsense. So following a consistent, appropriate style tacitly reassures the reader that the writer or an editor has done a quality-control check.

What's more, style conveys a subtle, cumulative meaning. For example, periodicals and organizations that exhibit a lot of respect for authority, of whatever kind, tend to capitalize more people's titles than irreverent outfits do. Staunchly American organizations may capitalize references to U.S. institutions and lowercase those of their foreign counterparts. The AP calls, for example, for *the U.S. Army* but *the French army*. (Its stylebook explains, "This approach has been adopted for consistency, because many foreign nations do not use *army* as the proper name.") The innumerable tiny style decisions that a person, a publication, or an organization makes add up to a point of view or an aesthetic. In other realms tiny decisions can add up to a politically conservative or liberal or radical or libertarian point of view; they can add up to an architecturally Gothic or Colonial or Victorian or modern or postmodern or ongepatshket aesthetic. And in each case, once the basis is established, deviations from it—inconsistencies, anomalies, and gaffes—are what people are most likely to notice: He's a conservative who believes in women's unconditional right to abortion? She commissioned a fresco for the ceiling of her modern house?? He spells out *Mount* in place names but not *Fort*???

So use a stylebook. Assuming you don't need it in your capacity as a member of a professional organization like the MLA or the AMA, here are some things to bear in mind:

Among the stylebooks I named a few paragraphs ago, *The Gregg Reference Manual* is wide-ranging and thorough but not as well known as *AP* or *Chicago,* so using it to win arguments will generally be more of an uphill battle; its reputation is strongest in the field of business communication. *The New York Times Manual* is excellent, but its most recent (second) edition was published in 1999, and a lot has happened since then—in particular, the events of September 11, 2001, and their many ramifications—so at least as a journalistic tool, unfortunately it is on its way out of date. *New York Times* staffers have online access to a continually updated in-house stylebook, but outsiders do not. *The Wall Street Journal Guide* differs little from the *AP Stylebook* except that it places more emphasis on business and financial terminology, so its greatest strength is in business journalism. *Wired Style* has a snappy mainstream reputation because of its introduction, consisting of ten tips on how to write with attitude, but it is primarily a glossary of computer and Internet terminology. And *Words Into Type* is a fine, comprehensive stylebook that, unfortunately, hasn't been updated in thirty years, nor is a new edition under way. So never mind how to render *9/11* and Arabic names—*Words Into Type* is hopeless on such longer-term concerns as bias-free language, how to cite electronic journals, and where to put line-break hyphens, if needed, in URLs.

Therefore, if you don't use a stylebook already and want one for general purposes, your best choice is probably *AP* or *Chicago.* These two, America's most widely used stylebooks, each have their strengths. *AP* believes in speeding writers, readers, and its users on their way; *Chicago* is erudite, magisterial, and deliberative, and it will help you to be so too—or at least to appear that way.

At a big bookstore or library you can almost certainly find the two of them (and probably a few other stylebooks) to compare. The AP's style is unfussy. For example, the stylebook doesn't even contain the word *footnotes,* let alone give you a preferred footnoting format. And the AP doesn't use diacritical marks, because "they cause garbled copy in some newspaper computers," according to the "Filing Practices" section of its stylebook. I've never dared ask Norm Goldstein, the book's longtime editor, if part of the rationale might also be that using diacritical marks consistently—in everything from words derived from French and German to the names of Latino ballplayers—would add a whole extra level of nuisance that reporters and copy editors on tight deadlines really don't want to deal with.

If the *AP Stylebook* appeals to you, buy the spiral-bound version available at www.apbookstore.com or, probably, at your local college bookstore, rather than the regular paperback version that's sold commercially. The AP's own edition costs less, you'll get the latest annual update, and the spiral binding lets the book lie open flat, so it's easier to use for reference.

You might alternatively, or also, consider buying an individual site license to get access to the *AP Stylebook* online. One advantage of doing this is that the site is continually updated, so if you often have questions about words and names that have just popped up in the news, you'll be more likely to find answers. Better yet, the site lets you personalize your version of the stylebook, annotating rules or even changing them and adding new ones. But the online stylebook also has some disadvantages. You have to be online to use it, of course. And it's very literal-minded. For instance, suppose you wonder whether it agrees with its house dictionary that *healthcare* is preferably one word. Type *healthcare* into the online stylebook's search window and you'll be told, "Your search found no results." Maybe *health-care*? Nope, again no results. Only if you type in *health care* will you elicit the entry "*health care* Two words." If you'd been looking in the printed book, you would have found what you wanted to know without ado.

Obviously, *AP* is aimed at journalists; *Chicago* is intended for people working on literary or scholarly books, periodicals, or articles. *Chicago* includes a whole chapter on foreign languages and the extra marks and characters they involve, and two chapters on footnotes, along with endnotes and bibliographies. It is updated only about once a decade—but now is a good time to get to know it, if you don't already. A new edition, the fifteenth, came out in the summer of 2003, so you can be confident that any rules you memorize now will remain in effect for a while. The manual covers a huge amount of territory, including electronic publishing and references thereto and the basics of usage.

Let it be said, though, that *Chicago* has the potential to drive you mad if, instead of deciding in advance to follow its primary recommendations, you prefer to make your own choices wherever it gives you choices. For instance, the fifteenth edition recommends that "all punctuation marks should appear in the same font— roman or italic—as the main or surrounding text, except for punctuation that belongs to a title or an exclamation in a different font." But that is called the "primary system" for deciding what font to use for punctuation, and an "alternative system"—a slightly more complicated one that was recommended in the previous edition— is also given. There is a well-thought-out discussion of how to form various kinds of possessives, but here, too, an "alternative" practice is offered, in this case a greatly simplified one. *Saint* in place names "may be abbreviated or spelled out in text." And *three* methods of using ellipsis points are explained. All these options do reflect intelligent standard practice in various quarters. But those of us who like to consult a stylebook so that we don't have to convene a council at work to decide (or sit alone, head in hands, and ponder) what rule to follow may be disappointed not to receive firmer guidance on matters like these.

Chicago also has a Web site, at www.chicagomanualofstyle.org. To get acquainted with *Chicago* before making a commitment to it, take a look at the site's Q&A section. It explains, "Even at nearly 1,000 pages, *The Chicago Manual of Style* can't cover every detail. In this forum we interpret the *Manual*'s recommendations and uncoil its intricacies," and it imparts *Chicago*'s advice on subjects ranging from abbreviations to word division. There's a place to submit questions for which you can't find answers either on the site or in the manual, once you're a *Chicago* initiate. And you'll be able to search the manual for paragraphs relevant to terms you're interested in. It would be too good to be true—since access is free—if it called up the relevant paragraphs onscreen; instead, it refers you to the manual, which you can buy directly from the site if you like.

From the Style File

Here are a few more stylebook-type questions, variations on which turn up in my mail fairly often.

"Should it be *a.m.* and *p.m.* or *A.M.* and *P.M.?*"

The traditional literary practice was to use *small* caps: A.M. and P.M. Employing a special font like that was and is too elaborate for newspapers, though, so newspaper styles generally call for lowercase letters. And now that word processors have, in effect, turned writers of many kinds of material into their own typesetters, generating small caps is becoming a lost art. (Do you use Microsoft Word? Click on "Format," then "Font," and then under "Effects" check the "Small caps" box. Thereafter what you type in lowercase will come out as small caps.) The current edition of *The Chicago Manual* evidences a slight preference for lowercase. It says, though, that *a.m.* and *p.m.* "may also be set in small capitals," and it goes along with a prevailing anti-clutter trend when it declares that with small caps "periods are unnecessary": AM and PM.

"I have a question about the use of *percent* or % in copy. The *AP Stylebook* and other style guides continue to advise using *percent* in copy and % in tables. I work for a Fortune 500 financial-services organization and can see good reason to let go of past practice and begin using % in copy. Many publications in the financial-services industry now use % in copy, and it is much more recognizable to readers. Use of % also would save space. Any comments?"

Actually, *AP* warns against ever using %, observing in its "Filing Practices" chapter that the symbol "rarely translates and in many cases cannot be sent by AP computers or received by newspaper computers." But *The New York Times Manual* allows the symbol to be used "with a figure in headlines, tables and charts." And *Chicago* says, "In humanistic copy the word *percent* is used; in scientific and statistical copy, or in humanistic copy that includes numerous percentage figures, the symbol % is more appropriate."

Long ago in high school journalism class I was taught that most people take in the word *percent* more efficiently than they do the % symbol. But your readers are in financial services, so surely the symbol is familiar to them. Citations in Nexis show that *Forbes* and *Fortune* both spell out *percent* when there's a spelled-out figure in front of it, as at the beginning of a sentence ("Twenty-eight *percent* of those surveyed . . . ") and when there's no figure at all in front of it ("a *percent* of sales"), but otherwise they use the symbol; and they seem to use % still more liberally in sidebars. Those might be good guidelines for you to follow.

While we're on the subject, may I impart my pet peeve about *percent*? Percentages are fairly precise—they are in effect fractions with a denominator of 100. When writers mean nothing more than "roughly half" or "one fourth," it seems to me that's the way they should put it—not "about 50 *percent*" or "some 25 *percent.*"

❖

"It is now common practice to lowercase the titles of high-ranking officials and dignitaries when they follow a person's name or stand alone. Thus one would write *the president, the pope, the queen.*

"How do you feel about sentences like the following? 'In her tour of the United States, the *queen* will visit *President Bush* in Washington.' 'On his next trip to England, the *president* will visit *Queen Elizabeth.*' 'The *president* also hopes to see *Pope John Paul II* in Rome, but it is not clear whether the *pope* wants to see *President Bush.*'

"Would it not look better if people of high standing had their titles treated the same way, whether the title preceded, followed, or stood apart from the person's name? Or am I the only one bothered by a capitalization guideline that confers importance on one dignitary and withholds it from another within the same context?"

I checked the *AP Stylebook, Chicago, The Gregg Reference Manual, The New York Times Manual,* and *Words Into Type,* and only *Gregg* is bothered by the inconsistency. *Gregg* advocates retaining the caps in the "titles of high-ranking national, state, and international offices when they follow or replace a specific personal name." But the others would all call the capitalization in your example sentences correct—though *Words Into Type* allows exceptions to the general rule to be made depending on "the nature of the publication."

Your rule admittedly makes it easier to treat important personages evenhandedly, but it creates problems of its own. First, we need to decide who is a capital-*P* Personage and who is just a regular person. And second, it becomes impossible to accord evenhanded treatment to people who lie on opposite sides of that line, wherever you draw it. *Gregg* draws the line beneath the level of "heads of government agencies and bureaus," ambassadors, "the Chief Justice of the United States," and state lieutenant governors. So its rule will result in sentences like "The Lieutenant Governor and the state attorney general are scheduled to confer this morning" and "George J. Tenet, the Director of Central Intelligence, discussed recruitment with John Hennessy, the president of Stanford University."

It seems to me the best way out of the morass is to keep the possibility of seeming to slight one party or another in mind and, wherever possible, edit sentences so that comparable personages receive comparable treatment: "On her tour of the United States, *Queen Elizabeth* will visit *President Bush* in

Washington." "On his next trip to England, the *president* will visit the *queen.*"

❖

"More and more, I see the word *The* used and capitalized in names, even in midsentence: for example, 'It was reported in *The Chicago Tribune.*' Is this *The* necessary? To me, it just looks high-falutin."

Speaking as someone familiar with the style of *The Atlantic Monthly,* I know as well as I know my own name (actually, better—but that's a long story) that *The Atlantic* considers *The* to be part of its name. Desiring to do unto others as we would have them do unto us, we go to the trouble of figuring out how publications we're citing or quoting from render their own names. It's the *Los Angeles Times* but *The New York Times,* the *Detroit Free Press* but *The Boston Globe, National Journal* and *National Review* but *The New Republic.* And, by the way, it's the *Chicago Tribune.*

As you might imagine, this is a nuisance to get right consistently—and for our pains we get a result that looks inconsistent. *AP* advises: "Capitalize *the* in a newspaper's name if that is the way the publication prefers to be known. . . . Lowercase *the* before newspaper names if a story mentions several papers, some of which use *the* as part of the name and some of which do not." That makes life a bit simpler. For once, *Chicago* would have it be simpler still. It says, "When newspapers and periodicals are mentioned in text, an initial *the,* even if part of the official title, is lowercased (unless it begins a sentence) and not italicized."

Still more of a nuisance is choosing to extend the "Do unto others" rule beyond publications to entities such as The Pew

Charitable Trusts and The McGraw-Hill Companies, which capitalize their *The*s. *AP* doesn't give clear guidance on this subject. It says, "In general, avoid unnecessary capitals," but it also includes *Newspaper Guild, The* in its list of formal union names and refers users to *Standard & Poor's Register of Corporations* to determine businesses' formal names. *Chicago* says bluntly, "A *the* preceding a name, even when part of the official title, is lowercased in running text."

"I find it slightly pretentious of some to insist on capitalizing the word *god* only when the god being referred to is the Judeo-Christian one. I always see *the Wiccan god* or *the Hindu god* and think it unfair. While I realize English matured in a Christian environment, it seems time for the language to stop giving implicit preference to one religion over another."

Stylebooks tend to agree with you. However, *AP* reminds us of an important difference between Christianity and Hinduism when it says "Capitalize *God* in references to the deity of all monotheistic religions. . . . Lowercase *gods* and *goddesses* in references to the deities of polytheistic religions." Dictionaries tend to make this distinction as well. But *Chicago* says, "Names of deities, whether in monotheistic or polytheistic religions, are capitalized."

Thus stylebooks take it for granted—or so I like to think—that we may each have our own answers to the question Whose God is the real God? As for Which style is the best style? it's up to us to find our own answers to that, too.

CHAPTER SIX

Read the Manual

When I was small, I would make what I thought of as innocent dinner-table conversation with my father by asking him things like "Daddy, what is existentialism?" (He was a philosophy professor.) He would respond, "Do you really want to know—are you willing to sit and listen to a half-hour lecture? Or do you want just a quick definition?" And he would give me whichever kind of answer I asked for.

I've told this, casually, to many people, most of whom have been nonplused by my father's response. I liked it, though. Those conversations went much better than the exchanges with my mother that started like this: "Mommy, what's an alveolar macrophage?" (She taught microbiology.) She would switch right into really-want-to-know mode, and go on and on, oblivious that dinner was finished and my brother and I were squirming in our chairs. Attempts to stop the flow of words with "OK, thanks—I guess I've got it" were met with "You asked, and I haven't finished telling you." I've grown up much more interested in philosophy than microbiology.

My father cared not only about philosophy but also about language. After his death, my mother gave me his copies of the original *Dictionary of Modern English Usage,* by H. W. Fowler, *Webster's Dictionary of Synonyms,* and *Webster's Third,* along with the dictionary stand on which this last, heavy tome had been enthroned. The books were well thumbed and, I discovered, annotated. Now, on my bookshelves, they still see use.

Why am I telling you this? Partly in order to draw a little analogy: If my father's field of scholarship had been English and what I'd asked him at dinner had been language questions, I think when I wanted the quick definition, he would have suggested I look it up in the dictionary. And when I really did want the whole story, we would have read a usage manual together.

Then, too, my favorite usage manuals remind me of my father. They're erudite, measured, sensitive to nuance, gently humorous, and kind—though they do not suffer fools gladly. They take it for granted that we want to better ourselves and that the means to that goal include education and a good command of language. The books I think of as most strongly imbued with those characteristics are Fowler's *Dictionary of Modern English Usage* (either the first edition, from 1926, or the second, from 1965, please) and *Garner's Modern American Usage,* by Bryan A. Garner, published in 2003.

Other fine usage books exist as well, and depending on your upbringing and disposition, you may feel more comfortable with them. (Actually, although none of us can have more than one father at a time, we're free to adopt as many usage books as we like.) Some have the tone of gruff newspapermen. Here I'm thinking of *The Careful Writer: A Modern Guide to English Usage* (1965), by Theodore Bernstein; *The New York Times Manual of Style and*

Usage, second edition (1999), by Allan M. Siegal and William G. Connolly, in its usage-manual guise; and *Lapsing Into a Comma: A Curmudgeon's Guide to the Many Things That Can Go Wrong in Print—and How to Avoid Them* (2000) and *The Elephants of Style: A Trunkload of Tips on the Big Issues and Gray Areas of Contemporary American English* (2004), by Bill Walsh.

Some other books want to assure us that everything we really need to know is simple—I'm thinking in particular of *The Elements of Style*, by William Strunk Jr. and E. B. White (it's on its fourth edition now, but any except the first, which lacks E. B. White's chapter on style, will do you). Yet other books take the point of view that learning what we need to know is not only simple but fun, fun, fun—for instance, *Woe Is I: The Grammarphobe's Guide to Better English in Plain English*, by Patricia T. O'Conner (1996, with an expanded edition published in 2003), and *The Deluxe Transitive Vampire: The Ultimate Handbook of Grammar for the Innocent, the Eager, and the Doomed* (1993), by Karen Elizabeth Gordon. You and I have outgrown these last two books, I suspect, but they make nice gifts for those we hope might follow in our footsteps.

Still other books whose opinions about usage I value, though I take them with a grain of salt, include *The American Heritage Dictionary*, for its usage notes (about which see Chapter Three), and *Merriam-Webster's Dictionary of English Usage* (1994), to be discussed later in this chapter. Wilson Follett's *Modern American Usage: A Guide* (1966, revised by Erik Wensberg in 1998) gets overwrought at times but says some sensible things I haven't seen elsewhere—for instance, about commas and about when to retain particles with French surnames (if you wonder why people say *De Gaulle* but *Tocqueville*, see "titles and proper names 5").

And *The New Fowler's Modern English Usage* (1996), edited by R. W. Burchfield, is the up-to-date product of enormous quantities of research, but I'm afraid I've taken a dislike to it. For one thing, its coverage of American usage is far more haphazard than Burchfield promises. Worse, Burchfield is trading on Henry Fowler's good name—*Fowler's* is in huge type on the book jacket and *Burchfield* much smaller—and yet he disparages Fowler shamelessly. From Burchfield's preface, for instance:

What I want to stress is the isolation of Fowler from the mainstream of the linguistic scholarship of his day, and his heavy dependence on schoolmasterly textbooks in which the rules of grammar, rhetoric, punctuation, spelling, and so on, were set down in a quite basic manner. . . . Perhaps as a hangover from Fowler's days as a schoolmaster, his scholarship needed to be enlivened by a veneer of idiosyncrasy and humour.

These assessments may even be accurate, as far as they go, but someone should have talked Burchfield out of publishing them, both because they seem mean-spirited and because they completely miss the point of Fowler, who does a better job than anyone else has done of demonstrating how to bring both rigor and good taste to bear on English usage.

Other books I'm glad to have handy are *A Dictionary of Contemporary American Usage* (1957), by Bergan and Cornelia Evans; *American Usage and Style: The Consensus* (1980), by Roy H. Copperud; and the *Harper Dictionary of Contemporary Usage,* second edition (1985), by William and Mary Morris. I refer to these less and less, though, because they've never acquired a popular following (hence the number of people willing to accept their judgments as authoritative is small) and, alas, they're going out of date. But if you find copies inexpensively at used-book stores, as I did, they are worth snapping up.

Twenty More Questions

The mid-twentieth-century voices in usage that remain particularly influential are Fowler's *Dictionary of Modern English Usage* (in what follows, I'll use the second edition, because that's the one people seem to have) and *The Careful Writer,* by Theodore M. Bernstein. I'll call these books Fowler and Bernstein, to reflect that the views expressed therein are those of the individuals named. It's true that the second edition of Fowler was edited by Sir Ernest Gowers, but Gowers, unlike some other people we might mention, considered his job to be updating the citations and streamlining the book's organization rather than supplanting Fowler's point of view with his own.

The most influential contemporary American voices are *The American Heritage Dictionary* (our old friend the *AHD*), *Garner's Modern American Usage* (which I'll call Garner, because it, too, represents the viewpoint of one person), *Merriam-Webster's Dictionary of English Usage* (*MWD*), and *The New York Times Manual of Style and Usage* (*NYT*). Full disclosure: I served as a consultant on Garner. That means I got to argue with Bryan when I disagreed with him, but ultimately either I brought him around or I didn't—his book calls 'em as he sees 'em. Also please note that a separate *American Heritage Book of English Usage* exists, though I'd rather have the whole dictionary; and that condensed versions of Garner's views on usage can be found in *The Oxford Dictionary of American Usage and Style* and in the 2003 edition of *The Chicago Manual of Style,* for which Garner wrote a new chapter on usage.

Now, gosh, let me think . . . Wasn't there a question in Chapter Two that I promised to finish answering in this chapter? Why, look—here it is again!

"My question is about *into* and *in to*. Are they interchangeable? Or are there times when only *in to* is correct other than when the *to* is part of an infinitive?"

Like dictionaries, usage guides show less interest in your question than in helping us distinguish between *in* and *into*. Still, two of our six guides do discuss *into* versus *in to*. *Merriam-Webster's Dictionary of English Usage* says, in part:

The adverb *in* followed by the preposition *to* is not to be confused with the preposition *into*. . . . [The mix-up] seems most likely to occur where *in* idiomatically belongs to the preceding verb and *to* goes with a human object. . . . [W]e find in the handbooks more than one illustrative instance of 'suspects turned themselves into police.' . . . It should be *in to*.

And Fowler simply declares, "The two words should be written separately when their sense is separate. Correct accordingly: *The Prime Minister took her* into *dinner. / All the outside news came* into *us immediately.*" That is, Fowler would have us change each of those *into*s to *in to*.

Also like dictionaries, usage guides, when they do discuss a subject, don't exactly speak in unison.

"Perhaps the use of the phrase *as well as* to mean 'and' or 'also' has been with us for a long time, but I have begun to notice it with high frequency in recent years. For some reason it bothers me to hear someone say 'I went to New York, Boston, *as well as* Philadelphia on my business trip.' Am I being picky?"

Maybe so—but join the club. *As well as* isn't just a long-winded way of saying *and*. Rather than joining elements of equal value, it gives less grammatical weight to the word or words following it than is borne by the ones that come before. This implies, by the way, that your example sentence needs to read ". . . New York *and* Boston as well as . . . " It also implies that if you were discussing only two cities, Boston and Philadelphia, the construction would be grammatically singular: "Boston, *as well as* Philadelphia, has terrific restaurants for business lunches." *As well as* carries a shade of meaning that *and* does not: it means something like "and not only." Your sentence, coming out of the blue the way it does, might be expected to elicit a response like "Did I know you were in Philadelphia?" If you had previously mentioned your visit to that city, though, your *as well as* would be fine.

I published that exchange in *The Atlantic*'s Word Court column, having learned years earlier from Eleanor Gould Packard, *The New Yorker*'s longtime copy editor par excellence, what I reported. And I reproduced it here expecting to go back and find at least some authoritative usage guides that agreed with me. (*The Atlantic*'s fact checkers don't just let me pop off; I always have to turn supporting documentation in to—yes, *in to*—them, though I can't remember what I gave them in this case.) The thing is, none of the leading usage books does fully agree. In discussing *as well as,* most guides focus on the form or number of a verb following *as well as:* "Boston as well as Philadelphia *was*" or ". . . *were*"? And "I work in the office as well as *go* on business trips" or ". . . *going* on business trips"? Garner—under *subject-verb agreement,* with a cross-reference under *as well as*—shares my view that what follows *as well as* doesn't affect the number of a verb. That is, he would call "Boston, as well as Philadelphia, *has* . . . " correct. But he doesn't say anything about what *as well as* means. Nor does *MWD*, though it goes on for more than a page about the number of the verb to follow (its advice, in a nub, is "Follow your instinctive feeling") and about the various uses to which *as well as* is put, as a conjunction and as a preposition.

A tiny digression: Grammarians, linguists, and lexicographers can wax on and on about whether a given term is a conjunction, a preposition, or both—but rarely do they stop to explain to other people why they're supposed to care. Once upon a time, saying that *as well as* can perform both functions would have been somewhat like pointing out, today, that a certain device can function as both a cell phone and a camera. We all understand what that means and what it implies about using the thing. But because grammatical terminology isn't widely understood nowadays, usage manuals can be as mysterious to us as descriptions of cell phones with built-in cameras would have been to people a few hundred years ago. Simple grammatical constructions and concepts can be explained in easy-to-understand terms, but when people start asking about anything tricky, answering them becomes . . . well, I sometimes wish I could follow my father's example and ask "Do you really want to know?"

Bearing in mind, however, that what we have here is the *written* word and that if you don't really want to know, you can skip ahead, I am going to follow my mother's example and tell you a whole lot about *as well as,* including why the difference between its conjunctional use and its prepositional use matters. When *as well as* is a conjunction, it connects grammatical equals—for instance, "I traveled from Boston to Philadelphia *as well as* from Philadelphia to New York." When it's a preposition, it attaches something subordinate to something that is closer to the grammatical core of the sentence: "*As well as* having to travel for work, I travel for pleasure." To use an analogy from a few hundred years ago, a conjunction is like a yoke beneath which two animals are paired, and a preposition is like a tether for one animal. I didn't have room to get into (yes, *into,* not *in to*) all that in the original Q&A about *as well as,* and besides, I was trying to spare readers the grammatical terminology. But if you look back, you'll see that I am, in effect, declaring *as well as* to be a preposition in my correspondent's sentence.

To return to our usage books: The *AHD* defines *as well as* as both a conjunction meaning "and in addition" and a preposition meaning "in addition to" and does not elaborate in a usage note—so it seems to be saying that "I went to New York, Boston, *as well as* [meaning 'and in addition'] Philadelphia on my business trip" is just fine, thank you. *NYT* comes closer to backing me up. It observes that "the phrase introduces what is essentially a parenthetical aside," and it does so in the course of explaining why what comes after *as well as* shouldn't affect the number of a verb. Thus *NYT* doesn't consider *as well as* to be a conjunction, because if it were, *A as well as B* would be plural.

Bernstein is with me on the issue of what *as well as* means: he says that "*as well as* is, technically at least, a conjunction meaning *and not only.*" But by calling it a conjunction Bernstein paints himself into a corner, as he admits, because he isn't ultimately in favor of treating *A as well as B* as plural. Fowler, much like Bernstein, says the meaning of the phrase "is not *besides,* but *and not only.*" Fowler, however (under *well*), insists that *as well as* is a conjunction and only a conjunction—which is not a view widely held nowadays. If we go back to our seven dictionaries, we'll find that only *The New Oxford American Dictionary* takes that line. A couple of the others define the phrase under *well,* so they don't have to assign a part of speech to *as well as*. And *Webster's Third* calls the phrase a preposition and an adverb, and not a conjunction at all.

None of my trusty usage sources says a word—at least, anywhere I could find—about one aspect of my correspondent's question which I answered without thinking twice about it. I and all of my books, I believe, would agree that there's nothing wrong with "I went to New York *as well as* Philadelphia." (We differ as to whether that means ". . . and not only Philadelphia" or ". . . and in addition Philadelphia," and whether *as well as* is a conjunction or a preposition there, but never mind—none of us finds the sentence grammatically deficient.) What the books don't address is the issue of "New York *and* Boston, as well as Philadelphia," as I recommended to my correspondent, versus "New York, Boston, as well as Philadelphia," the way he wrote it. In the former formulation, *and* is, as usual, a conjunction, leaving *as well as* to be a preposition. In the latter, *as well as* sure acts like a conjunction—but this is grossly unidiomatic, no?

Telling yourself that you know what's idiomatic and what isn't is, of course, an easy way to get into (not *in to*) trouble. But how can I be sure that what sounds right to me really is right? Let's look in the Nexis database, which, again, consists largely of material that has passed muster with professional editors. As of this writing, every single citation from the past five years that involves a series of cities including New York, Boston, and Philadelphia, and that has an *as well as* in or next to the series, puts an *and* before the term preceding *as well as*. For instance, from *The New York Times:* ". . . symphony orchestras—Chicago, Philadelphia, Boston, Cleveland *and* New York, *as well as* great European ensembles." So I was right about the idiom here, and the main thing left to argue over— again, there is no consensus—is whether *as well as* means "and not only," as I was taught, or "and in addition."

And maybe that's enough about that. But haven't we, a mere two questions into this chapter, reached the point about usage books that it took most of Chapter Two to reach about dictionaries?

- It's necessary to understand some grammatical terminology in order to take in what usage books are saying.

- It helps to keep an open mind about where they may be saying it (in different books, discussions of *as well as* appear under the phrase itself, under *well,* and under *subject-verb agreement*).

- Even the most authoritative books don't always address exactly what we're interested in.

- When they do answer our question, they give widely varying advice.

Are you beginning to feel alarmed that the preceding heading was "Twenty More Questions"? Tell me about it! Yes, my mother's daughter has written this chapter. And my father's daughter's advice is: If you're more interested in the specific usage questions and answers than in how the usage books sort themselves out, just skip all the text that looks like the present paragraph. But if you'd like to know about usage manuals, too, read on. My correspondents will ask me questions, I'll say what I think, and then we'll discuss what usage books say, roughly in the order of the strictest view first and the most permissive last, occasionally including sources other than our basic six. That's the organizing principle, and I'm mentioning it because I wouldn't be surprised if you were unable to figure it out on your own.

My Mother's Daughter, Continued . . . and Continued and Continued

"In nearly every current book I read, the author has somewhere benightedly used the word *crescendo* to describe an arrival rather than a process. For instance, in the *New York Times* best seller *In the Heart of the Sea,* by Nathaniel Philbrick, I read, 'Their physical torments had reached a terrible *crescendo.*' As a professional musician, I take umbrage. *Crescendo* is a term meaning to travel from, say, a pianissimo to a fortissimo, and at the end of a *crescendo* one might be said to have arrived at a *climax.*"

Thanks for spelling out the problem so clearly. Although the likes of F. Scott Fitzgerald and P. G. Wodehouse have written *crescendo* where they meant the peak rather than the approach to it, a number of language authorities frown on this usage.

The *AHD,* Bernstein, Garner, and *NYT* all agree with my correspondent and me; Fowler is mute on this point; and *MWD,* while not denying that the word more traditionally and commonly means "gradual increase," says, "The 'peak, climax' sense of *crescendo* . . . is clearly a fully established meaning."

This result, and even subtleties thereof, could almost have been predicted by someone generally familiar with these books. The *AHD* labels the meaning "the climactic point" a *"usage problem"* and explains why in a note. But before reporting that 55 percent of its usage panel rejected an example sentence in which *crescendo* carries this meaning, it observes, *"Crescendo* is sometimes used by reputable speakers and writers to denote a climax or peak, as in noise level, rather than an increase. Although citational evidence over time attests to widespread currency . . ." Typical!

Bernstein, Garner, and *NYT* don't pussyfoot around. You can open any of these books, readily find a warning against using *crescendo* to mean "peak," and be on your way. As for Fowler and his failure to comment, well, he is elderly—long dead, to tell the truth—and British. The *Oxford English Dictionary* gives as its earliest citation for the disputed usage, "The caterwauling horns had reached a crescendo. . . ," from *The Great Gatsby*, published in 1925. Again, the first edition of Fowler was published in 1926 and the editor of the 1965 edition added few wholly new entries. So the disputed usage of *crescendo* was brand new in Fowler's time, and it was coming from the United States, whose idioms Fowler did not claim to know. Burchfield's *New Fowler's*, by the way, says, "In origin the word is the present participle of L *crescere* 'to grow'. . . . The new use still lies rawly in disputed territory, eschewed by anyone knowing the meaning of the Latin participial ending."

MWD, the odd book out on this question, is often the odd book out, for good reason. Painstakingly researched and richly detailed, it is also adamant that its role is to report evidence from published sources, not to opine or crusade. (From its flap copy: "*Merriam-Webster's Dictionary of English Usage* is intended to serve the reader or writer who wishes to go beyond the personal predilections of a particular commentator or the subjective pronouncements of a usage panel.") Now, I, as you'll recall, feel strongly that the consensus of informed opinion is more significant than the thoughts that happen to float off the top of my head—so you might think I would be in sympathy with *MWD*. Besides, who am I to tell F. Scott Fitzgerald that he's an ignorant git for using *crescendo* the way he did in *Gatsby*?

I can only cite my years of hands-on experience with the work of many hundreds of writers, much-lauded and otherwise. If I had been assigned to read galleys of *Gatsby,* I would have marked Fitzgerald's *crescendo* and written in the margin, "In Latin, this means 'growing.' Maybe 'The caterwauling of the horns was deafening'?" And there's a good chance that the author would have either OKed the change or come up with another, better way of saying what he meant. As a writer *I* make mistakes; *I* don't know everything; *I* am grateful when weaknesses in my work are pointed out before they get into print. I'm no Fitzgerald, but delicate fingerprints of mine appear on the work of beloved writers published in *The Atlantic Monthly* in the late twentieth century, and a few of those writers have even gone out of their way to thank me for the service I did them.

And so I believe that the "consensus of informed opinion" can't be determined by what even the best writers do. What we really want to know is what they *would* do if they had the benefit of a well-informed specialist's advice. Fowler and Garner each tend to say, Here's what I think, and here's why—and the reader can find their arguments persuasive or not, and go along with their recommendations or not. *MWD* tends to say, Here's what published writers do; their choices are all over the map; one option is as valid as the next. That may well be true, but as I said at the outset of this book, it isn't the kind of advice that anyone I know seems to want.

❖

"Which is correct: 'If better relationships with customers and partners *are* your goal' or 'If better relationships with customers and partners *is* your goal'?"

The number of a verb should always match the number of the subject, not the complement. So *are* is correct in that clause. If the sound of that makes you wince, you could turn the

clause around and make *goal* the subject: "If your goal *is* better relationships . . . "

I couldn't find a usage note in the *AHD* about this one way or the
other, but everyone else agreed with me, Bernstein and Fowler under
number, NYT under *number of subject and verb,* Garner under *subject-verb agreement,* and *MWD* under *agreement, subject-verb.*

Most usage manuals, including all of our six, are organized dictionary style. (Indeed, one of them is actually a dictionary.)
Nonetheless, usage guides are less straightforward to use than dictionaries per se, because often, as just now, we want to know about
a concept rather than a word—and the relevant information can
pop up in unexpected places. If you're seeking the word *subject* in
the *AHD* or any other dictionary, you know just where to look for
it: after *subjacent* and before *subjection* or *subjective.* But if you're
wondering about subject-verb agreement, will your usage manual
(or the *AHD*'s usage notes) discuss it under that heading or *agreement, subject-verb;* or *number;* or what? Furthermore, since it's not
certain where a given topic will be covered, it can be hard to figure
out whether a given book covers it at all.

Fowler didn't do us any favors when he imparted practical advice under such whimsical headings such as *battered ornaments*
and *unequal yokefellows.* But because readers had grown fond of
them and knew what they referred to, Gowers allowed many such
amusements to remain in the second edition. Burchfield has un-
ceremoniously dumped most of them—and that annoys me, naturally, though if you aren't already a Fowler follower, you probably
won't mind.

A bright spot amid the murk is that usage manuals (and dictionary usage notes) are cross-referenced, so if you make a halfway

plausible guess about where to find what you want to know, you are likely to be led, eventually, to the proper place—assuming there is one. I'm sure that in a few of our usage books I have missed clearly stated answers to a few of the questions here. All I can say is that even with the best will in the world, and knowing the terminology likely to apply, I often couldn't find in usage guides what I imagined I would, any more than a few chapters ago I could find every nicety I sought in dictionaries.

(Note to reference-book marketing departments: If usage manuals were on CD-ROM or online, carefully cross-referenced and searchable in various ways—as, for instance, the *Oxford English Dictionary* is—how much more useful they'd be! When I began my career as an editor, I didn't mind spending ten minutes or so riffling through Fowler to find an entry I remembered having seen in there somewhere, and then spending another five minutes reading the relevant section, in order to answer a question about one word or phrase in copy. As time has gone on, though, this has come to feel more and more like having to yoke up the oxen and drive the oxcart to the library whenever I want to look something up.)

❖

"I have been searching for years for a learned opinion regarding the correctness of not using an apostrophe with the pronoun *ours*. Various high school English teachers have provided varying answers to this query. Please reply with some advice."

Egad! The next thing you know, English teachers will start having varying opinions about the correctness of the spellings *your's*, *her's*, *hi's*, and *their's*. Possessive pronouns don't use apostrophes: *ours* is correct, along with *mine, yours, his, hers, its,* and *theirs.* The possessive case of nouns does use them: *our friend's* is correct, along with *my friend's* and *your friend's.*

Everyone would already know this, you'd think, if only the study of grammar were taken more seriously. For years, though, I have been hearing anecdotal laments that "they don't teach grammar in the schools anymore." Not long ago David M. Bloome, who was then the president-elect of the National Council of Teachers of English, told me that grammar does receive less class time than it used to, and he explained why: a great deal of research has shown that most schoolchildren who are taught grammar neither remember what they've learned nor become better writers than children who aren't taught grammar. Or, to borrow an analogy from Samuel Jay Keyser, a professor emeritus of linguistics at MIT, who used it to make much the same point to me, "If I wanted to teach kids to swim, I wouldn't give them a course in hydrodynamics; I'd put them in the pool and have them practice swimming."

All the same, if I wanted to be the most effective possible swimming *coach,* I might find it helpful to know something about hydrodynamics. Bloome and Keyser go along with that. Keyser told me, "The grammar of *ours* is actually fascinating. Although *ours* and *our friend's* are parallel in your examples, note that you can say *our friend's book* but not *ours book.* An English teacher who is interested in things like this will be a better teacher than one who isn't."

Garner says, "*Ours,* an absolute possessive, is sometimes wrongly written *our's,*" and gives three citations that illustrate the mistake. I couldn't find anything on this point in Bernstein or *NYT.* Fowler, under *our,* discusses *our* versus *ours,* taking it for granted that *ours* (as opposed to *our's*) is the correct form. The

AHD, in its entry for *ours*, makes clear how the apostrophe-free word is used. *MWD* says, "The possessive pronoun *ours*, like the possessive pronouns *its*, *theirs*, and *yours*, is properly spelled without an apostrophe"—and when *MWD* issues a definite pronouncement like that, everyone had better listen up.

❖

"When I was a student teacher in a middle school, my master teacher's pet peeve was the popular use (or misuse) of *it's* as a contraction of *it has*. I see this usage daily: '*It's* been a tough day' or '*It's* been a pleasure meeting you.' It sounds wrong to me, too. Is it?"

No—at least not when *has* is used as an auxiliary verb. (Compare "My car needs a tune-up; *it has* trouble climbing hills," which can't be shortened to "... *it's* trouble...," with "*It has* always had trouble climbing hills," which contracts nicely into "*It's* always had trouble ...") And you'll want to keep in mind that since *it's* can be a contraction of either *it is* or *it has*, in some contexts *it's* will be annoyingly ambiguous. (Does "It's left" mean "It *has* left" or "It *is* left"?)

Sad to say, these days the distinction between *it's*, the contraction, and *its*, a possessive, needs defending. "My car ran out of gas and one of *its* tires went flat—*it's* completely ruined my day." Surely the reason this distinction gives people trouble is that the possessives of pronouns don't use apostrophes (*its*), whereas the possessives of nouns do (*car's*).

Where the superstition got started that *it's* is legitimately a contraction only of *it is* is unclear to me, but I suspect that the fault may lie with usage guides so concerned to draw a clear distinction between *it's* and *its* that they forget to mention that *it's* can mean *it has* as well as *it is.* And sometimes usage guides object to the overuse of contractions generally. But I've never seen one that actually forbids the use of *it's* as a contraction of *it has.* Your master teacher was being what's called overnice.

And that's the view from here. Garner, under *its, it's,* says, "The contraction for *it is* is *it's.*" But nowhere does he say that *it's* should not be used for *it has*—and he gave himself a golden opportunity to do so, if he cared to, with an entry headed *contractions, ill-advised forms.* And at least once (in the entry for *dare*) he uses *it's* to mean *it has:* "*It's* been called . . . " *NYT* says, "The contraction *it's* means *it is* (or, less often, *it has*)." Fowler and Bernstein don't discuss this. And the *AHD* and *MWD* say that *it's* can mean either *it is* or *it has.*

❖

"As an English major, with a graduate degree (M.A., English literature), and as a lover of the language, I find it increasingly shocking that in virtually every 'knowledgeable' magazine article or story, I see the misuse of the possessive. For example, 'He is a friend *of Frank's.*' The correct use of the possessive, as I recall, is that the apostrophe substitutes for the word *of.* That is, 'He is a friend *of Frank,*' or 'He is *Frank's* friend.' But to say 'He is a friend *of Frank's*' is ridiculously, tautologically redundant, not to minimize its offensiveness to those of us in the know."

Would you say "a friend *of him*"? Double possessives like "a friend *of Frank's*" may be "freaks of idiom," as Fowler deemed them, but idiomatic they are; Shakespeare's *Antony and Cleopatra* begins, "Nay, but this dotage *of our general's* o'erflows the measure." Possessives, including the word *of,* do jobs besides in-

dicating relationships of possessing or having. The examples
with which grammarians like to demonstrate this point often involve the word *picture* or *portrait:* "a picture *of Frank's*"—a picture that Frank possesses—is different from "a picture *of Frank.*"

When, exactly, should we use double possessives? This is controversial. My rule is to experimentally substitute a pronoun for the
noun, as I did at the outset of this reply; if I'd say "a friend *of his,*"
then I say "a friend *of Frank's.*"

All of our six usage sources, under *of* or *possessives* or (unless
you've studied a classical language, you'll never guess) *double geni-
tive,* stand up for the double possessive. None of them, though, offers a clear line of demarcation between when this construction is
necessary and when it is undesirable.

"Is it incorrect to interchange the meanings of *anxious* and *eager?*
It seems *anxious* implies nervousness and *eager* implies desire.
Nevertheless, many use *anxious* to describe desire, and dictionar-
ies often describe the two words as synonyms."

These words overlap to a degree. *Garner's Modern American
Usage* says: "Today the word [*anxious*] typically encompasses
both worry and anticipation. . . . The word carries a sense of expectation. . . . [W]hen no sense of uneasiness is attached to the
situation, *anxious* isn't the best word." I concur. So if I said I was
anxious to persuade you of my point of view, that would be plausible, but if I said I was *anxious* for the workday to be over so that
I could put my feet up and relax, that would be odd.

Bernstein, too, wants careful writers to use *anxious* only where
some degree of anxiety is involved. And *NYT* agrees: "*Anxious*

means uneasy or worried. Avoid the less precise sense, as a synonym for *eager*." A usage note in the *AHD* begins, "*Anxious* has a long history of use roughly as a synonym for *eager*, but many prefer that *anxious* be used only when its subject is worried or uneasy about the anticipated event." *MWD* gives numerous citations and concludes, "Anyone who says that careful writers do not use *anxious* in its 'eager' sense has simply not examined the available evidence." And Fowler—out of keeping with his reputation as a defender of traditional distinctions—says that using the word in the sense of *eager* is a "natural development . . . almost universally current." Who'd've thunk?

❖

"The latest issue of your *Copy Editor* newsletter contains the following: '*CE* found that by a margin of nearly five to one, newspaper and magazine references in the preceding two months did not . . .' Shouldn't this be *ratio* instead of *margin*?"

Right you are, and thanks for reading the newsletter so closely! According to *The New York Times Manual,* "*margin* means, among other things, the difference between two values. So a candidate who wins an election with 8,000 votes when the loser got 5,000 has a *margin* of 3,000. That candidate did not win *by an 8-5 margin* or *with a margin of 8,000 to 5,000.*"

Although the *AP Stylebook* doesn't say anything about margins, it says about ratios: "Use figures and hyphens: *the ratio was 2-to-1, a ratio of 2-to-1, a 2-1 ratio. . . .* Always use the word *ratio* or a phrase such as *a 2-1 majority* to avoid confusion with actual figures." Thus it implicitly makes much the same point as *NYT.* The *AHD* defines *margin* as "a measure, quantity, or degree of difference: *a margin of 500 votes,*" and *ratio* as "relation in degree or number between two similar things"—thus also making the point. None of our other main sources discusses this question.

❖

"My co-workers and I are faced with a dilemma. In the sentence 'If your child does not wear glasses, please contact us so we can remove [blank] name from our list,' the nagging question is how to fill in the blank. Previously we would have used the universal *his* or *his/her*. *His/her* seems too politically correct to us and can get repetitive. We hear it is becoming acceptable to use the word *their,* but that is grammatically incorrect, since *your child* is singular. Please help!"

I am almost ready—not quite, but almost—to accept the idea that words like *everyone, anyone,* and *no one* may be thought of as plural. At least, "*Everyone* should bring *their* glasses to school that day if *they* wear glasses" is how about nine out of ten people would express that thought in speech these days. The problem, though, is that if you rearrange the words a bit, you end up with "*Everyone* who *wears* glasses should bring *their* glasses to school," and there the verb that goes with *everyone,* namely *wears,* is singular while the pronoun, *their,* referring to it is plural.

There are words (say, *couple* or *sheep*) that can be either singular or plural—but any given instance of any given word is supposed to be one or the other, and for good reason. Keeping straight what's going on in something like "Has anyone who tutors children in reading lost his or her glasses?" is tough enough when you can trust the numbers of the verbs and pronouns to match the nouns they go with.

In your sentence, with its singular *child,* I would urge you not to give in and use *their.* How about either *his or her* or *the child's?*

Or you could recast the sentence as "If your child or children do
not wear glasses, . . . remove their names . . . "

NYT is resolute: "*Their, theirs, them, they.* These pronouns are
plural. Do not apply them to singular antecedents (like *anyone* or
someone) even when the aim is to avoid assuming maleness or fe-
maleness; other solutions exist." Bernstein expresses much the
same view—unsurprisingly, because for many years he worked as
an editor at *The New York Times.* He says, "The thing to do is
change the antecedent, making it [collective or plural]. This is no
ignominious defeat because nothing has been lost; it is rather a
facing of the facts of syntax." Fowler argues in favor of but doesn't
insist on the convention of using masculine pronouns in sentences
like my correspondent's—as was standard until two or three
decades ago. He adds (this is about as snide as Fowler ever gets),
"Have the patrons of *they* etc. made up their minds yet between
Everyone was *blowing their noses* (or *nose*) and *Everyone* were *blowing their noses?*"

Garner says, "Where noun–pronoun disagreement can be
avoided, avoid it. Where it can't be avoided, resort to it cautiously
because some people may doubt your literacy." That seems to be
the gist of the *AHD*'s advice as well. An *AHD* usage note reads:

The use of the third-person plural pronoun *they* to refer to a singular noun
or pronoun is attested as early as 1300, and many admired writers have used
they, them, themselves, and *their* to refer to singular nouns such as *one, a person, an individual,* and *each.* . . . Most of the Usage Panelists reject the use of
they with singular antecedents. Eighty-two percent find the sentence *The
typical student in the program takes about six years to complete their course
work* unacceptable. Thus, the writer who chooses to use *they* in similar con-

texts in writing should do so only if assured that the usage will be read as a conscious choice rather than an error.

And *MWD* says: "*They, their, them* are used in both literature and general writing to refer to singular nouns, when those nouns have some notion of plurality about them. . . . Notional agreement is in control, and its dictates must be followed."

"As a teacher, I keep correcting student writing that uses *can not* as two separate words when the student would appear to mean *cannot.* I have seen this mistake in other nonpublished writing, such as bank letters. Could you please address the difference between 'I *cannot* tell a lie' and 'I *can not* tell a lie'?"

Cannot rules out a possibility; *can not* implies that one has a choice. I take it you don't let your students use contractions. Still, you might tell them that if they can mentally substitute *can't* without changing the meaning, then they should write *cannot.* There is an exception to this rule, though. *Cannot* may turn into two words when an affirmative idea intervenes: "I *can* cheerfully obfuscate but *not* tell a lie." In truth, *cannot,* there, would read better than *not.* But in shorter sentences *not* is idiomatic: "I *can* taste but *not* smell"; "I *can* drink but *not* eat."

Garner's view is that "*cannot* should not appear as two words, except in the rare instances when the *not* is part of another construction (such as *not only . . . but also*)." The *AHD* calls *cannot* "the negative form of *can*" and refrains from giving *can not* as an alternative spelling. Neither Fowler nor *NYT* discusses this question. Bernstein—to my astonishment—says, "The one-word form is preferred unless the writer desires to put special emphasis on the *not*," and gives as a correct example of this (uncommon) device: "This company can tolerate human mistakes; it can not tolerate sabotage." *MWD* says, "Both spellings are acceptable, but *cannot* is more frequent in current use," and, like Bernstein, mentions that the parts of the word may be separated for emphasis.

❖

"I heard an announcer say, 'Jackie Robinson had his number retired by all major-league clubs, and *rightfully* so.' I distinguish between *rightfully* and *rightly.* Am I right to do so?"

Yes, you are. The distinctions that dictionaries draw between the two words are at best blurry and confusing, but in good usage *rightly* is the opposite of *wrongly,* and *rightfully* means much the same as *by rights.* In saying *rightfully,* that announcer used the wrong word.

Garner, under *right,* says, "*Right* = correct, proper, just. . . . *Rightful* = (1) (of an action) equitable, fair <a rightful solution>; (2) (of a person) legitimately entitled to a position <the rightful heir>; or (3) (of an office or piece of property) that one is entitled to <his rightful inheritance>." Bernstein, Fowler, *MWD,* and *NYT* say nothing about a distinction. The *AHD* says *rightly* means "in a correct manner; properly: *act rightly*" and "with honesty; justly," and that one of the meanings of *rightful* is "right or proper; just"— so evidently it would not find fault with what the announcer said.

❖

"One bit of linguistic ignorance that cries for attention is the use of *may* when *might* is meant. I once heard a TV anchorman say that 'one bullet aimed at Hitler *may* have saved millions of lives.' '*May* have'? As if there's still a chance that those millions of people survived Hitler? And my local newspaper once reported that an unfortunate judge who was killed when a block of cement fell on him *may* still be alive had he not walked where he did at the wrong moment. When I read that, I felt like alerting his family so that they could have his body exhumed and examined."

As a verb, *might* is really just the past tense of *may.* But the issue here is not that Hitler and your unlucky judge both belong to the ages: note that the wording of "Hitler *may* have been the most heinous tyrant in history" is perfectly correct. A past-tense verb like *might,* besides talking about what has already happened, can be used to talk about things—past, present, or future—that are wholly hypothetical. The past tense, that is, can express the subjunctive mood. For instance, "if wishes *were* horses" isn't about past wishes but is about wishes that are not and never will be horses.

Might has long been used in ways that would be hard to predict from reading about the subjunctive in style guides and basic grammar books. Consider "I *might* start volunteering at the homeless shelter" and "*Might* I be of service?" In these sentences, which nearly everyone would consider correct, *might* simply expresses a bit more uncertainty or deference than *may* would. So the boundaries between *might* and *may* are not staked out clearly. Yet there remains a difference—as you know. *Might* is the only proper choice when talking about hypothetical things that did not happen—as in both your examples—or possibilities in the present or future that cannot happen: "If wishes were horses, beggars *might* ride."

MWD says it's "stumped" about why *may* sometimes appears where *might* "would have been expected." (Note that wording—

not "would have been correct.") It also says there's "nothing mysterious or controversial about . . . the words' basic uses" and refers anyone with questions to "a good dictionary." The *AHD* does, it seems to me, cover the spectrum of the words' uses adequately. Fowler and *NYT* don't discuss this point. But Bernstein and Garner consider *may* versus *might* to be a mite more complicated than *MWD* says it is. From Bernstein:

May poses a possibility; *might* adds a greater degree of uncertainty to the possibility. . . . Occasionally, the flippant understatement of casual conversation may reverse these roles of the two words. The man at the cocktail party who says, "I might have one more drink," means he would like it pronto. But if he says, "I may have one more drink," he does not necessarily mean that he wants it immediately and he may be debating whether he wants it at all.

❖

"Everywhere I go, I hear people saying 'I wish I *would have* done X' instead of 'I wish I *had. . . ,*' or 'If I *would have* done X' instead of 'If I *had . . .*' It strikes me as grammatically wrong, but I am at a loss for a technical explanation of why it is—or isn't—a mistake. I wish I had taken an English grammar course more recently than eighth grade!"

An assertion that contains *would have* is contingent on something. For instance, "I *would have* washed it *if . . .* " something else had or hadn't happened—"if I *had* known you were going to eat it," let's say. But how can the event on which our contingency rests be contingent as well—"if I *would have* known you were going to eat it"? (In your mind, strip away the *if* from that and consider what "I *would have* known . . ." by itself means, and the problem will be obvious.) Similarly, contingency is bound up in the very idea of a wish, as in your first example, so following *wish* with *would have* is in effect redundant: good grammar calls for "I wish I *had* known you were going to eat it."

I suspect that when *would have* appears in an *if* clause and the *if* clause precedes the main clause, as in your second example, the speaker or writer has made the mistake by thinking ahead to the contingent part. I've heard at least two other explanations, though, for why this mistake is as common as it is. Possibly some people who have heard such contractions as "If I'*d* seen you in time, I'*d* have stopped you" have gotten the first '*d*, which stands for *had*, garbled in their minds with the second one, which stands for *would*. Or possibly people are extrapolating from *could have*, which (because its underlying verb, *can*, behaves differently from *would*'s underlying *will*) isn't necessarily wrong in similar constructions—say, "If I *could have* washed it, I would have."

Under *would have*, Garner says that "*would have* for *had* is an example of a confused sequence of tenses," and gives relevant examples. Bernstein, under *subjunctives*, says a bit that heads in that direction, and *NYT*, under *conditional tenses*, does too, though its entry is explicitly about *if* sentences. Fowler and the *AHD* are unhelpful. *MWD*, under *would have*, says:

The use of *would have* in place of *had* in the protasis of a conditional sentence (as in "If they would have come earlier, we could have left on time") has been cited as an error in books on usage since at least 1924. . . . Our evidence indicates that it does not occur in standard writing that finds its way into print, but it is notorious in student writing and therefore a staple of college handbooks even today.

Google News, though, begs to differ with *MWD* about whether the error shows up in print. The month's worth of news I recently searched contained almost 250 instances of *if I would have* where *if I had* belonged—and that's without my having bothered to count *if you. . . , if he. . . , if she. . . ,* and *if they . . .* citations.

❖

"In a practice book for the ACT Assessment, I came across the following sentence: 'The children have gone fishing for the day.' I was supposed to say whether or not the sentence was correct. I thought it was. However, the authors of the book said that the sentence was incorrect, because a perfect verb must be followed by an infinitive. I have never heard of this rule, and neither has my English teacher. We combed through Fowler's under every heading we could think of but could find nothing. Does this rule exist?"

Any student and teacher who rush to Fowler's *Modern English Usage* for answers to their language questions deserve at least a gold star and possibly a medal. If you look under *gerund* in the second edition of Fowler, you'll find a few paragraphs about "gerund and infinitive" that aren't exactly on point but come pretty close. You'll want to read the whole passage, but the nub of it, I think, comes when Fowler says "There is very little danger of using the gerund, but much of using the infinitive, where the other would be better." Throw that practice book out!

When I first plucked that question out of my mailbag, I imagined it was just the kind of thing about which I could rely on usage manuals' support. But looking up *perfect verb, infinitive, gerund,* and I don't know what all else in usage books got me scarcely any further than looking words up in a dictionary. The *AHD,* among its definitions for *go,* gives "To engage in: *went skiing.*"

The people who wrote that practice book were evidently think-ing of constructions like "I *have wanted to know* about this for a long time" and "I *have gone to look* it *up* in my reference books." But the sentence they concocted is more nearly on the pattern of "I *have wanted information*" and "I *have searched* my *books*." In "The children have gone fishing," *go* is a transitive verb (meaning that it takes an object) and *fishing* is a gerund, or a noun derived from a verb, serving as the object.

"I do not profess to be very knowledgeable in the field of grammar, so many grammar rules puzzle me. Recently I heard from a trusted source—namely, my English teacher—that the word *not* should be avoided when a person is writing something formal, such as an English essay. This was annoying, given that *not* is quite a useful word, and hard to avoid. The reason was that passive sentences should be avoided, and adding *not* to any sentence makes it passive. I have never heard this before. Please explain."

Yikes! If that really is what your teacher has been telling you, may he or she enjoy a glorious retirement, and soon. No more in grammar than in everyday life are "passive" and "negative" the same thing. We'll have to wait until another time to talk about the passive voice in grammar. A rule against using *not* in formal English is news to me. Is it possible that your teacher was sim-ply encouraging you to write in a not unstraightforward manner—that is, plainly?

After that exchange was published, I received this comment:

"Like you, I cringed when I read the tangled comments from the student on not using *not*. But I teach MFA fiction students, and I find myself encouraging them to render statements in the positive form (unless there's a compelling reason to do otherwise); generally, you save words and sound more confident. I stole this directly from the venerable Strunk and White's *Elements of Style*—still good advice: 'Put statements in positive form. . . . Use the word *not* as a means of denial or in antithesis, never as a means of evasion.'"

Good point. Garner, under *negatives,* warns, "Double negatives such as *not untimely* are often used quite needlessly in place of more straightforward wordings such as *timely.*" Fowler (under "*not* in meiosis and periphrasis"—uh-oh!) says, "The right principle is to acknowledge that the [*not un-*] idiom is allowable, and then to avoid it except when it is more than allowable." *MWD* remarks about constructions of that kind, "When this device is overused, reviewers and commentators on style can get annoyed." I couldn't find anything in the *AHD* or *NYT.* Bernstein, though he warns against superfluous *not*s that create unintended double negatives (as in "It would not have been surprising if the Governor had not reappraised his personal and political plans"), seems unperturbed by "deliberate double negatives designed to produce understatement ('Adultery is not infrequent among this tribe')."

"I've noticed that in certain publications this type of construction is frequently used: '*The* installation artist John Adams, who is married to *the* poet Sally Brown, said recently that the state of arts funding in New York has become dismal in recent years.' I'm wondering about the *the* that precedes the person's occupation. I've noticed that this construction is used only when the writer is referring to certain occupations.

"One theory I have is that it is used by convention to dignify these occupations, and by implication it denigrates others when it is not used. For example, one will see '*the* sociologist Dr. Peter Jackson' but very rarely '*the* lawyer Susan Johnson,' and never '*the* accountant Alex Smith.' And one will also never see any of the trades referred to in this way: '*the* cement finisher Bill Collins,' '*the* garbage collector Mike Thompson.' What light can you shed on this? My instinct is to say that this construction betrays a certain classism, but I leave such lofty conclusions up to you.

[Signed]

"The starving graduate student"

The point is actually not class but fame. I don't think of *the cartoon character Dilbert,* for example, as a high-toned guy, and yet it seems appropriate for me to refer to him here with that phrase. The construction suggests that I believe you've heard of Dilbert but you might still like a little hint to help you place him. Contrast the phrase *Dilbert, a cartoon character,* which is likely to leave you either feeling faintly insulted, because of course you've heard of Dilbert, or convinced that I must be really out of it not to know that he's a household name.

I would, though, be likely to introduce *Breakup Girl, an online superhero,* with *that* phrase, the implication being that I'm not surprised if this is the first you've heard of her. Our language can also readily suggest a third degree of fame: extreme. Extremely famous people and characters need no introduction. That is, I would be inclined to say simply *Spider-Man* or *Betty Boop,* in the full expectation that the name alone is enough to call one of these characters to mind.

Garner essentially backs me up, under *titular tomfoolery,* where he quotes *NYT* approvingly: "Only official titles—not mere descriptions—should be affixed to names. Do not, for example, write *pianist Lynn C. Arniotis* or *political scientist Tracy F. Baranek.* But in a reference to someone well known, a descriptive phrase preceded by *the* is acceptable: *the sociologist Merrill H. Cordero.*" I found nothing in the *AHD,* Bernstein, Fowler, or *MWD* under *the* or *titles* or *names* or *appositives* or *descriptors* or *first references.* Under *coined titles,* Bernstein protests against constructions like "West 135th Street scrubwoman and subway rider Anna Johnson," in which *scrubwoman and subway rider* is being treated as if it were a title, like, say, *Officer* (for a member of the New York City police force) or *Senator*—but Bernstein says nothing about *the.*

❖

"In recent years a number of publications have indulged in a habitual, almost ritualistic reversal of the familiar *from . . . to* sequence. I think this practice started in the business press ('The stock declined yesterday *to* $.09 *from* $116.32 in light trading') and spread to other media from there. As a reader encountering such phrases, I often feel I'm being knocked to post from pillar. Can you help discourage such awkwardnesses before things go to worse from bad?"

You're not the only person to have written me about this seeming trend. Most of the citations I've found that illustrate it are indeed from the business press. Surprisingly, in the media in general the likes of *increasing to* and *decreasing to* are actually more common, respectively, than *increasing from* and *decreasing from.* But after most of these *to* phrases no *from* ever turns up, so the sentences give no cause for complaint.

Language doesn't promise to present events or ideas in chronological order, but when it brings us things in reverse chronological order, as *to . . . from* tends to do, the writer or speaker ought to have a good reason and provide ample signposts to make clear what he or she is doing. Otherwise, as you've neatly demonstrated, the result can be disorienting. Some people who write *to . . . from* imagine, I think, that they are calling attention to the word that comes first. And in a sentence like your hypothetical example, which concludes with a bland prepositional phrase, maybe they are. Still, "The stock declined in light trading yesterday *from* $116.32 *to* $.09" would be an improvement, because as usage authorities are fond of pointing out, ordinarily the most emphatic place in a sentence is the end.

When *The Atlantic* was getting ready to publish this question, it occasioned a minor panic among the copy-editing staff. A copy editor, Linda Lowenthal, recalled having seen a message on a copy-editing listserver (if you're enjoying this book, you might like to sign yourself up for it, at listserv.indiana.edu/archives/copyediting-l.html) to the effect that the *AP Stylebook* recommends the *to . . . from* order. It doesn't in fact. But Linda asked her CELmates (as people who subscribe to the listserver refer to themselves) if they had seen any such rule anywhere. Kind copy editors checked dozens of sources and found nothing—nor did I—until at last one turned up this snippet from the two-page-long *numbers* entry in *NYT:* "When reporting a rise or fall, give the *to* figure first (in spite of logic), to prevent misreading as a range: *In a week, the stock rose to $25 from $17.75.* And *The price fell to $850 from $998.*"

Well, I said to myself, one usage manual's recommendation about rises or falls in things numerical isn't enough to change my mind about the overall point. Furthermore, the example my correspondent gave ("declined . . . from $116.32 to $.09") is impossible to misread. I was, however, glad to learn what people who write *to . . . from* sequences might conceivably have in mind.

❖

"I find it hard to be curmudgeonly with someone who is trying to be polite to me. Yesterday the young man at the customer-service counter met me with a sincere smile and an ungrammatical question: *'How may I help you?'* That evening I heard the same question from a telephone operator in an ad for a major credit card. I can tell you *how* you *can* help me or *that* you *may* help me, pure and simple. As for *how* you *may* help me, I'm really at a loss for words. To my ear, *'How may I help you?'* just sounds dumb.

"Given the number of interactive situations between service employees and the public (stores, call centers, government agencies), this may be the most ubiquitous linguistic error in English-speaking North America."

Although most of us were taught that *can* refers to ability to do something, and *may* to permission, the two words have always overlapped somewhat, particularly in informal speech and in negative constructions, *mayn't* being clumsy to say. Time was, however, when the overlap that curmudgeons complained about was the informal use of *can*—in, for example, "*Can* I help you?" (to which a curmudgeonly response would be "How should I know whether you can? All the same, please try"). Honestly, I think the problem with *How may I help you?* (which means "What manner of help do I have your permission to offer?") is that it's redundantly polite, a quality I just can't bring myself to object to.

After I published that exchange, a reader sent me the following:

"'*How may I help you?*' isn't redundantly polite; it is taught in sales- and service-type job-training courses as a question to which a potential customer cannot answer no. Here's the scenario, as it is taught: A customer walks in, the salesclerk asks 'May (or "can") I help you?,' the customer replies 'No.' End of conversation, because the clerk has nowhere to go with that.

"When the salesclerk asks 'How may I help you?,' the theory is, the customer cannot respond 'No' to the question. Therefore, so goes the theory, there's no end to the conversation—though there is one very rude response that can end the conversation quickly. It goes something like 'By effing off.'

"I've always been put off by the 'How may I' question ruse. It isn't a normal greeting, it's a canned question, right up there with 'Would you like an apple turnover with that?'"

Point taken. I've made an attempt to see what usage manuals might have to say about this issue—but they don't say much. Fowler's and Garner's entries headed *commercialese* were the closest I came. These, however, are about such stilted phrases as "enclosed please find" and "in the amount of" that too often turn up in businesspeople's correspondence. Garner quotes *How to Do Business by Letter,* by Sherwin Cody: "The test of a word or phrase or method of expression should be, 'Is it what I would say to my customer if I were talking to him instead of writing to him?'" Here, no doubt, the test needs to be updated to "Is it anything I would say to this person if I were off duty?" But I'm afraid we've left usage behind and entered the territory of spin.

"In an interview with Steven Pinker I read recently, he said, '. . . need not undermine ideals like morality and human equality.'

Instead of '*like* morality and human equality,' shouldn't he have said '*such as* morality and human equality'? I've heard some editors say that *like* is OK to use this way because the reader understands what is being said. However, couldn't this be true of several other errors in writing? The reader understands the word *ain't,* but it is not correct. The reader understands *I would have went,* but it is not correct. Shouldn't *such as* be used to delineate or explain? Shouldn't *like* should be used as a comparative term?"

Well, but nobody maintains that *ain't* and *would have went* are good English. My own view is that using *like* where *such as* would convey the same meaning is perfectly good English unless in a given context *like* is ambiguous. As an analogy, think of *if not.* No one calls it incorrect. Yet authorities often warn writers and editors to take care that the reader will be able to tell what it means. Compare "This subject comes up often, *if not* every day" (so does it come up every day?) or "This subject is controversial, *if not* earth-shatteringly important" (no need to be sarcastic!).

Bill Walsh, in *Lapsing Into a Comma,* admits that the distinction between *like* and *such as* "is ignored by many fine writers," but says, "I think it is worth observing: The phrase *players like Borg, Connors and McEnroe* can be read as excluding the very players it mentions." Fowler and Garner don't discuss *like* versus *such as,* and neither does Bernstein's *Careful Writer,* though Bernstein in a different book, *Miss Thistlebottom's Hobgoblins: The Careful Writer's Guide to the Taboos, Bugbears and Outmoded Rules of English Usage,* calls the difference between the two terms "slight." *MWD* says, "The issue of ambiguity, which evidently underlies the thinking of those who urge the distinction, is probably much overblown." The *AHD* gives as one of the definitions of *like* "such as; for example: *saved things like old newspapers and pieces of string*," and comments no further. And *NYT* explicitly favors *like* over *such as*. It says, "*Like* is the preferred expression . . . in this kind of phrase: *painters like Rubens*." Under *such as*, it explains, "In introducing an example (*multinational companies such as Coca-Cola*), the phrase is stilted."

"Is it all right to call someone a *co-chairwoman* when the other person doing the chairing is a man—presumably referred to as *co-chairman*? My friend and I have been arguing about this. He maintains that *-woman* is an integral part of the title, and that therefore unless the person's counterpart can be identified in the same way, it is objectionable to incorporate into the title the component *co-*. But I contend that gender is in this case incidental, and is used only to expand on the attributes of the individual filling the role. Which is it?"

If we as a society are really heading toward gender equity and yet sometimes find women in positions of authority identified as *chairmen,* maybe it would be good for the male sex if its members were every now and again identified as *chairwomen,* or *co-chairwomen.*

Just kidding. Isn't the situation you're describing exactly what the word *co-chair* is for?

There is often, by the way, reason to look askance at the prefix *co-,* as your friend is doing, for it is regularly used where it is useless. (What's wrong, for instance, with "He and she will be the *chairs* of the committee this year"?) But here *co-* isn't any part of the problem. At any rate, you can't stay out of trouble by referring to the two people together as *chairwomen*—or *chairmen.*

It seems that the question my correspondent asked doesn't come up often. Although most of our sources weigh in on sexism and *chairman* and *co-* and so forth, the only one with any halfway relevant advice here is *NYT,* which says, "Avoid *co-chair* (noun and verb)." For nouns, it recommends *chairman* and *chairwoman* instead, which may sound old-fashioned, but the advice comes with a clear, thoughtful, contemporary warning against sexual stereotyping.

❖

OK, I admit it: that wasn't twenty questions but twenty-one—more than you bargained for. I allowed myself to dawdle among the usage books because I've learned and continue to learn so much from them. In fact, these are books from which we learn how to think about English. They are an essential tool in the kit of, arrow in the quiver of, subroutine in the computer program of, handbag in the closet of . . . what metaphor appeals to you? Word people rely on usage manuals. And now our tool kit, our quiver, our computer, our wardrobe, is almost complete. We just need to take stock of a few special-purpose items and we're in business.

CHAPTER SEVEN

Special-Purpose Tools

"Three of my grandchildren, ages four to ten, were discussing the expression *for the love of Pete*. Can you tell us who Pete is and how this phrase came to be symbolic of frustration? The whole family is happy they have chosen the phrase in preference to some of the more modern statements that language offers."

Pete, in this phrase and also in *for Pete's sake*, isn't a person but a forerunner of political correctness. *For the love of Pete* was coined exactly so that people could use it in preference to less polite equivalents. As *The Oxford Dictionary of Slang*, by John Ayto, explains, the name is "a euphemistic substitute for *pity*, itself used in oaths in place of *God* and *Christ*." The slang dictionary's big sister, the *Oxford English Dictionary*, contains several citations for *Pete* used in this way. The earliest of them is from 1924 and is American.

I was so happy when that question turned up in my e-mail in box! Not only is the question appealing, but the answer wasn't hard to find; I could explain it straightforwardly, using reliable sources; and the answer was even—it seemed to me—interesting. My editor at King Features Syndicate also loved the question, and he had his heart set on my using it to kick off the weekly newspaper version of Word Court that was soon to begin. But the woman who had written the letter had neglected to tell me what town and state she lived in, and it's an absolute requirement for the columns that people tell me their full names and where they live, and give me some way of verifying that information—in part to prevent someone who dislikes you from asking a really idiotic question and signing your name to it for all the world to see. I sent my correspondent an e-mail, then two, asking for the missing information. But the deadline for the first newspaper column was approaching and I hadn't heard back.

Fortunately, my correspondent had an unusual last name. So, using an online telephone directory, I set to work finding all the households in the country with that name and calling them up. Within three calls I'd found the woman's niece, who promised to ask her aunt to get in touch—and at last she did.

Tools for Antiquing

Why go to so much trouble? Why not just pick another letter, whose author had followed all the rules, and move on? Well, I know that people are interested in word-history questions; I certainly get lots of them. But it is a rare word-history question that can be answered definitively in a way that won't put readers to sleep. As one of America's leading lexicographers told me recently, the more interesting the answer to a word-history question is, and the larger the number of pop word-history books and Web sites repeating that "information," the likelier it is that it's wrong.

Do you want to *know* where words and expressions come from? If you believe they are quotations or literary references, we'll discuss what to do a few pages further on. If not, then you should look them up in the *Oxford English Dictionary* (the *OED*)— preferably the online edition, which is continually corrected and updated—or the *Dictionary of American Regional English* (the *DARE*), whose four volumes to date cover *A* through *Sk;* or the *Historical Dictionary of American Slang,* by J. E. Lighter, whose two volumes to date cover *A* through *O;* or *I Hear America Talking* or *Listening to America,* by Stuart Berg Flexner; or *Speaking Freely,* by Flexner and Anne Soukhanov. That's the complete list of wide-ranging word-history books I (almost) trust. You might also try Googling (if you're looking for a phrase, put quotation marks around it and then add, not in quotes, *etymology*) and see what you get. But unless you find a source that looks like a dry academic listserver, which quotes from one of the books I just named or otherwise incorporates a lot of serious-minded, pointy-headed detail, the odds are that you've found a "folk etymology," too good to be true.

Real etymology is a painstaking discipline—it's the archaeology of words. If your neighbor came over, excitedly brandishing a shard of pottery that he'd found as he planted his garden and spinning an elaborate theory about it, you'd be, at best, amused, right? If you were kind and he was gung-ho, you might suggest he take it to the local historical society, to see what the people there could make of it. If *they* thought it might be something significant, they would probably pass it along to someone more authoritative for an opinion. Real word histories are like that, and quite often the best-informed answer possible is "Nobody knows where that came from." This doesn't stop people from speculating, of course.

❖

"Why are people who attend meetings called *attendees* and not *attenders*? The same goes for *conferees*. *Honorees* are people who are honored; *employees* are people who are employed. Why are these other two different?"

The simple answer is, They just are. English is inconsistent.

If you enjoy knowing about word histories, however, you may like this answer better: The English suffix *-ee* originated in the French passive-participle ending that we still see in the likes of *née* (feminine) and *fiancé* (masculine). I started to enlist *The American Heritage Dictionary* to back me up on this point, quoting from the usage note that explains, "The suffix *-ee* was first used in English to refer to indirect objects and then to direct objects of transitive verbs." But the first example the usage note gives is *donee*—which according to both the *OED* and *Merriam-Webster's Collegiate* pre-dates the verb *donate* by two or three centuries. Since the noun *donation* came first, *donee* doesn't actually demonstrate the process described.

No one disputes that Americans have long been more enthusiastic and less strict coiners of *-ee* words than the British. The *OED* clearly considers *attendee* an Americanism, giving the word's entry in *Webster's Third* (1961) as its earliest citation. *MWC*'s lexicographers, however, have found a citation from as long ago as 1937. And by the way, *attender* also appears in dictionaries, though nowadays it rarely makes it into print.

As for *conferee,* it, too, is an Americanism, but *MWC* traces this one all the way back to 1771. In the following 1779 citation from the *OED,* you'll notice it seems as if at that time *conferees* were thought of as people who came together to confer, rather than as mere attendees at conferences: "The *conferees* of Congress gave this committee very ample assurances of the disposition of Congress to preserve the most perfect harmony."

As you see, I checked *MWC* for dates. Merriam-Webster, whatever else I might say about it, evidently has a fabulous citation file. Sometimes Merriam-Webster will have found an earlier first appearance of a word than the *OED;* I believe this is particularly common for Americanisms. But, alas, *MWC* gives you only the date; it does not include historical citations, the way the *OED* does.

"According to *Merriam-Webster's Collegiate Dictionary,* eleventh edition, the phrase *tooth fairy* first appeared in the year 1962. I wasn't alive then, but I've talked to people who insist that they remember using the phrase prior to this date. Since the ninth and tenth editions also say 1962, it seems unlikely to be a typo. Could the tooth fairy really be so young? And what does Merriam-Webster count when researching a word's history? Only printed instances? Or does the staff look at film, radio, television?"

If truth be told, the tooth fairy who visited me is a bit older than the one who made herself known to Merriam-Webster. But as it says in *MWC'*s own front matter:

The printed date should not be taken to mark the very first time that the word . . . was used in English. Many words were certainly in spoken use for decades or even longer before they passed into the written language. The date is for the earliest written or printed use that the editors have been able to discover. This fact means further that any date is subject to change as evidence of still earlier use may emerge, and many dates given now can confidently be expected to yield to others in future printings and editions.

That is, surely one of these days a reader for Merriam-Webster will find an earlier citation. In the meantime, the *OED* is no help, because it gives *tooth fairy* only under *tooth,* as a combining form, without a citation. And the term doesn't seem to be an Americanism, nor is it exactly slang or colloquial, so our other trusty sources can't help either.

Do keep in mind that all dictionaries, even the *OED,* are works in progress.

"A week or so ago I saw this expression in the online edition of the *Chicago Tribune:* 'She *is friends with* the mayor's wife.' I couldn't believe my eyes. In fact, when I went to look up the citation in print to send it to you, it had been changed to 'She is *a good friend of . . .* ' Did 'The World's Greatest Newspaper' get it wrong in the first place, or did it fix something that wasn't broken?"

What for our current purpose is the World's Greatest Dictionary, the *OED,* contains citations for forms of *be friends with* that date back as far as Shakespeare: "I *am good Friends with* my Father" is in *Henry IV.* The sentence you read online is therefore hardly unprecedented. It's not obvious from the *OED* entry, however, where the phrase came from or how it fits into our language, so I asked the dictionary's principal philologist, Edmund Weiner, if he had anything more to share about the quirky *be friends with* idiom. Usage, he explained, seems in the sixteenth century to have slipped from *make* [someone] *a friend* to such less logical constructions as *hold friends with, make friends to,* and *be friends with.* By now most of these except *make friends with* and *be friends with* have dropped out of use. The revision of the *OED* that is now under way, Weiner says, will illustrate the progression in some detail.

❖

"Will you do battle with a usage error already deeply rooted in our dictionaries? I refer to the expression *pull oneself up by one's bootstraps,* generally defined as 'to help oneself without the aid of others; use one's resources.' This is flat wrong. Visualize the action. The pull exerted upward by one's hands is *precisely equal* to the pull exerted downward by one's feet. It is a Buster Keaton skit—a comical demonstration not of self-reliance but of stupidity. The phrase belongs not with examples of virtuous effort but with examples of futility, like trying to catch the wind in a net or trying to get blood out of a turnip."

Now that you've mentioned it, I'll never again be able to hear this expression in the same way. And yet most people, including such writers as James Joyce and Doris Lessing, who are cited in the *OED,* use it to mean what the dictionary says it does. Probably the expression would mean what you wish it did if its origin were in physics terminology rather than in literature.

Incidentally, did you know that it is the basis for the computer term *boot*? The *OED* demonstrates this, too. As early computer engineers saw it, when the instructions that were loaded first into the machine told it what instructions to load next, even a computer was able to pull itself up by its "bootstraps."

❖

"Recently a friend of mine referred to the phrase *to be in the same boat with (someone)* as 'inherently denigrating.' I guess this person figured the phrase has its roots in the slave trade, but I disagree. Can you settle this dispute?"

If people don't stop assuming the worst of every word and phrase, I'm going to scream. Here's a 1584 citation from the *OED,* penned by one Thomas Hudson: "Haue ye pain? so likewise pain haue we; For *in one boat* we both imbarked be." *In the same boat* has nothing to do with slavery and is not at all derogatory.

❖

"I have come across a new phrase, and I wonder if you have any insight into its meaning. I never heard it in New York City, but since moving to Virginia I have heard two people use *feeling froggy.*"

As the *Dictionary of American Regional English* project got under way, some four decades ago, researchers set to work administering language questionnaires to people all over the country. In 1969 an item about how a person who was "feeling in the best of health or spirits" might complete the sentence "I'm feeling ____" elicited the word *froggy* from a respondent in Georgia. Although the expression has never especially caught on, you'll be interested to know that over the past few years *feels froggy* appeared in the New York *Daily News* and *feeling froggy* turned up in *USA Today,* among other papers. As might be expected with slang or informal language that doesn't have wide currency and can't be found in most dictionaries, the expression's meaning, um, hops around a bit from one user to the next. Not only can *froggy* mean "chipper" or "frisky," as the *DARE* defines it, but in recent citations from news sources it often seems to be conveying an idea more nearly akin to "restless" or "lucky."

After that was published, I received this letter:

"Feeling froggy? You bet, but I have found it to mean more than 'chipper' or 'frisky': 'ready for a fight,' to be exact. Ever since my older brother brought the term home from his stint in the U.S. Marines forty years ago, it has been the 'Dare you' response to a challenge for a fight."

And this one:

"I have been a bar-band drummer for thirty years and have heard the phrase *feeling froggy* literally hundreds of times and always in the same context—as a component in an invitation to fisticuffs. Typically, 'You *feeling froggy,* son? Jump!' (that is, 'If you wish to fight, start swinging').

"It could be argued that my understanding has been stilted by . . . uh . . . the company I keep. I can only attest that the phrase is vigorously alive and, 'least down roun' these parts (Memphis, Tennessee), invariably explicit."

And this one:

"I have another idea about the origin of the phrase *feeling froggy.* When asked how he was feeling that day, my grandfather, a life-long resident of southwestern Virginia, used to say that he felt *'as fine as frog hair.'*"

And this one:

"Amongst our acquaintances here in southeastern Wisconsin the expression *feeling froggy* is used to describe one's having a bit of

chest congestion that slightly affects the voice, presumably derived from *having a frog in one's throat*."

See my point when I say it's no simple matter to figure out
where words and expressions come from—or even what they
mean now?

A somewhat different kind of word-history question relates to expressions that seem to have come from somewhere in particular. Here
the sources worth checking are more various. Quotation dictionaries
and computer databases, for instance, are likely to come in handy.

"Lately I have heard on radio and TV and seen in print this oddity:
The proof is in the pudding. For example, *The Wall Street Journal*
recently quoted Sandra Thurman, who had been President Clinton's AIDS czar: '"It's wonderful that they're going to keep the
[White House AIDS] office open," she said. "But *the proof is in
the pudding.*"' What do you suppose this means? Have the people
who say it never heard or read *The proof of the pudding is in the
eating*? Or does the newer phrase have some other meaning that
I'm just not hip enough to get? It's becoming more prevalent and
must be stopped before it's too late."

You're right about which expression is the original one; according
to *Bartlett's Familiar Quotations,* it comes from *Don Quixote,* by
Miguel de Cervantes. Nonetheless, the shorter version is hardly
brand new: in online archives it is easily found in newspapers
and magazines from some twenty years ago. Context usually
makes clear that the shorter version is intended to mean what
Cervantes's saying obviously does—fitting conceptually between,
oh, say, "Seeing is believing" and Aesop's "Nature will out," a

few thoughts down the way from *"Que será será."* There's really only one reason, then, to object to the shorter version, although this reason is compelling: *The proof is in the pudding* doesn't make any sense.

❖

"A recent issue of *The New York Times* included the following passage: 'Critics wonder whether the new digital film revolution for home computers merely *gilds the lily* of passive entertainment.' I had thought the correct expression to be 'To gild refined gold, *to paint the lily.*' Has common usage changed this quotation so that *gild the lily* is now the accepted version?"

Gild the lily is seen in print much more commonly than *paint the lily,* and where the latter does appear, often it will have been invoked just in order to let readers know that the original line is as you say and comes from Shakespeare—*King John,* to be exact. If not that, then the writer may quote the entire line and work in a mention of the Bard, thus self-consciously averting questions about word choice.

Gild versus *paint* therefore presents anyone who wants to use a version of the phrase with a dilemma, in the traditional sense of *that* word (namely, as the *AHD* has it, "a situation that requires a choice between options that are or seem equally unfavorable or mutually exclusive"). The problem was wonderfully sketched by the poet and critic Randall Jarrell, in a passage I discovered when the linguist Geoffrey Nunberg quoted it in his article "The Decline of Grammar," published in *The Atlantic* two decades ago. Jarrell, describing a literary character, wrote:

She always said *to paint the lily:* she knew that this was a commonplace phrase and that the memory of mankind had transfigured it, and she was contemptuous of people who said *to paint the lily*—just as she was contemptuous, in a different way, of people who said *to gild the lily*—but she couldn't bear to have anyone think that she didn't know which one it really was.

My own, cowardly solution to the dilemma is a third possibility not touched on by Jarrell (despite the Greek prefix meaning "two," a majority of the *AHD*'s usage panel permits a dilemma to have three or more possible solutions): I avoid using either version of the phrase.

"Several times lately I have seen the expression *God is in the details.* I've also seen the expression *The devil is in the details.* For example, today on page one of *The Washington Post,* a member of the National Security Council is quoted as saying that *'the devil's in the details here'* with regard to the deployment of a United Nations force. I suppose one could argue either case, but which is correct?"

Leaving theological issues aside, with an expression like this what is "correct" is a matter of whether one version came into being as a garble of the other. (Or, inasmuch as the two aren't used interchangeably, one might have begun as an allusion to the other.) Possibly this has happened here—but no one seems to know which version came first. Neither *God is in the details* nor *The devil is in the details* has a clear provenance. Though the former is occasionally seen attributed to Albert Einstein, Gustave Flaubert, and Friedrich Nietzsche, among others, the architect Ludwig Mies Van Der Rohe most often receives credit. Evidently Mies did say it, but he was not the first, and the latest edition of

Bartlett's Familiar Quotations (2002) attributes the saying to "Anonymous."

Bartlett's does not list *The devil is in the details.* Other sources name various personages as the popularizer, if not the coiner, of this version, but the range of them is narrower and more political—for example, the diplomat Paul Nitze, Ronald Reagan, and H. Ross Perot. Until the 1990s both versions of the saying were relatively rare, and neither was particularly more common than the other. As I discovered by rooting around in Nexis, however, about 1992—the year Perot began to be widely quoted, during his first run for the presidency—*the devil* began pulling out ahead of *God* in popularity. In February of 1993 Perot complained that the devil was in the details of an economic plan of President Clinton's, and he made headlines; others' use of the *devil* version of the saying has been on the rise ever since. Over a six-month period last year U.S. newspapers and newswires invoked the devilish saying more than a dozen times as often as they invoked the godly one.

"I was told that the term *crowbar* was racist. My co-worker said it was derived from *Jim Crow,* and that the device was named as such because it was used for menial labor. He said the appropriate term is *prybar.* Any insight?"

I truly am glad there are well-meaning people who stand up against racism, but I wish they were all well informed, too. According to the *OED,* in about 1400 the already existing word *crow,* for a bird, took on the additional meaning of an iron bar, "usually with one end slightly bent and sharpened to a beak." (Other sources say that the allusion may have been to either the bird's beak or its foot.) Shakespeare used the word *crow* in this sense—in *The Comedy of Errors,* as it happens: "Well, Ile breake in: go borrow me a *crow.*" People started adding *bar* to the name of the tool in the eighteenth century.

So is racism implicit in the fact that the bird that gave the *crowbar* its name is black? No. But does the fact that the bird is black have something to do with the historically derogatory term *Jim Crow*? Yes. According to Stuart Berg Flexner's *I Hear America Talking,* "Blacks were first called *crows*" in the 1730s, and this helped inspire a minstrel named Thomas D. Rice, in 1828, to write the song "Jim Crow" (sample lyrics: "My name's Jim Crow, / Walk about, and turn about, / An' do jis so"). The song's title eventually became shorthand for an era of overt segregation.

By the way, *pry bar* (two words) is in only one of the seven current American dictionaries I checked for you: the *New Oxford American.* The others say that *pry* alone can be used to mean "crowbar." But why not say *crowbar*?

That last paragraph elicited the following response, whose author makes a good point. I've omitted his comprehensive citations, some of which were from a 1978 book titled *Tools and How to Use Them,* by Albert Jackson and David Day, and others of which were links to particular pages in online catalogs where tools are sold, like www.sears.com and www.stanleytools.com.

"I read your June piece on the history of the crowbar with both interest and amusement. You stated that *pry bar* is synonymous with *crowbar.* I suggest that instead of consulting standard dictionaries for your definitions you might consider researching what is said and used in the field.

"A *pry bar* is a short, flat tool used for prying up nails, separating layers of nailed boards, and other lightweight tasks. A *crowbar* is a hexagonally shaped bar of heavy steel used to gain leverage in moving or separating heavy objects. If you wanted to lift one end of a wall to place a shim underneath, you would use a crowbar. If you wanted to remove the trim from the wall, you would be better off with a pry bar, as the crowbar would tend to gouge large holes in the plaster or Sheetrock.

"Confusion arises in that there is a cousin of the crowbar, the *ripping bar,* or as it is also known the *construction bar.* The classic crowbar has a fine point on one end and a chisel shape on the other. The ripping bar has claws on both ends, similar to a pry bar but maintaining the shape and strength of a crowbar. Truth be told, the ripping bar is often called a *crowbar,* as it is much more common and classic crowbars are rarely seen nowadays. While ripping bars are called *crowbars* (although not vice versa), they are never called *pry bars.* If a colleague asks for a crowbar while straining to lever a 200-pound steel I-beam into place and you proffer a 10-inch pry bar, you will soon learn the difference."

I am guilty as charged. When you're interested in specialized terminology—whether it's medical, legal, or construction-industry-related—specialized resources will serve you best. Another of my correspondents made this general point brilliantly:

"The recent discussion of *crowbar* brought to mind an oddity that has long astonished me. While a good resource like *The American Heritage Dictionary* proclaims its roster of 'Special Contributors and Consultants,' it is painfully clear that experts from many fields of daily life were not invited to try out for the team. You'll find an authority on Philosophy, but none on Cooking; a specialist on Turkic Languages, but none on Hardware. Or Farming. Or Building Trades.

"I offer this assortment of black holes purely by way of example: each such omission makes me wonder how many kindred common terms are missing.

- *Appaloosa* and *Clydesdale* gallop through the *American Heritage; paint horse* does not.
- My wife and I just bought an *orbital sander,* but my dictionary won't buy it. Nor has it heard of *finishing nails.*
- I doubt that you'll often have need of a *cooper,* a *fletcher,* or a *wheelwright.* But when you build your dream home, you'll surely want a *sheetrocker* or two. The old-time craftsmen make the dictionary; our contemporary does not. (An even stranger construction omission is *rebar.*)
- The South loves *hopping john,* and every western supermarket sells *masa harina.* But neither term is to the taste of my dictionary.
- A very different instance of regional lapse is the boxy cooling and humidifying device used throughout the arid West. Millions of westerners rely on *evaporative coolers,* or *swamp coolers,* yet these leave the lexicographers cold. Which in turn leaves me asking how many implements well known in Maine or Michigan have been excluded.
- Tens of thousands of miles of American roads, parks, farms, and ranches—plus endless fields, pastures, or other divisions within those parks, farms, and ranches—are bounded with fence that is attached to metal posts. Often painted dark green with silver tops, these *T-posts* are sold in countless stores—as are *T-post pounders* for driving them in and

T-post extractors for removing them. Simply, *T-posts* are one of the most common American roadside artifacts. But you've already guessed where no one has managed to insert one.

"Dr. Johnson famously defined *lexicographer* as 'a harmless drudge.' By way of addendum, I wish to offer a definition for *modern lexicographer:* a person who can tell you what a *fabricant* is and what *fabricable* signifies yet who has apparently never heard of *fabric softener.*"

Bravo!

Tools for Treasure-Hunting

There are, however, such things as general-reference books intended to help you get to know certain kinds of specialized terminology. And I happen to think leafing through them is a pleasanter way to while away an hour than reading *Tools and How to Use Them* or *Stedman's Medical Dictionary.* Sometimes we all find ourselves groping after the right word to describe, say, "the mantel over the window" or "the underbelly of a duck." A quick look in a regular dictionary will make clear that *mantel* does not usually signify the top of a window frame—so what *is* that thing called? What part of a duck is its *underbelly* presents no mystery, but unless your dictionary is illustrated and contains a bird diagram, it won't help you settle whether someone knowledgeable about birds in general, let alone ducks, would use that word. Unfortunately, there are few faster ways to give the impression that you don't know what you're talking about, particularly if you're talking to people who *are* well informed about a subject, than getting the lingo wrong.

Enter the visual dictionary and the reverse dictionary—each a trove of information intended to solve word problems of just these kinds. Visual dictionaries consist primarily of pictures of everything from, say, galaxies to cells, buildings to books, with the parts labeled. Reverse dictionaries start with meanings: to answer the *mantel* question, for instance, a user would look up *window* and would there be presented with a range of window-related words and their definitions.

I rounded up all such current reference books that I could find, except visual dictionaries intended for children, and I tested them with a number of questions, including the former two, to probe their strengths and weaknesses. The books I explored are *The Firefly Visual Dictionary* (2002); the *Ultimate Visual Dictionary* (2003); the *Reader's Digest Illustrated Reverse Dictionary* (1990); the *Random House Webster's Word Menu*, by Stephen Glazier (1997); and *Bernstein's Reverse Dictionary*, by Theodore M. Bernstein, revised and expanded by David Grambs (1988).

On the *mantel* question, both the *Firefly* and *Ultimate* visual dictionaries led me to the word *lintel*, but in each case I had to enlist the help of a regular dictionary to get there. Labels in pictures of various buildings, from periods of history as distant as that of ancient Rome, suggested I might want any of several terms—for instance, *quoin, architrave,* and *casing.* However, none of the other terms, except possibly *head of frame,* was apt, according to my regular dictionaries.

I found the *Illustrated Reverse Dictionary* easier to use for this question. The alphabetically ordered entries included *window,* under which a few dozen window-related words were proposed. These included *lintel,* which the book defined as "upper horizontal beam or support, as of a window." Eureka! The *Word Menu* also eventually led me to *lintel,* though in its "The Home" chapter I had to look beyond the list of words relating to "Windows, Walls, and Facades" and study "Ornamental and Structural Parts." *Bernstein's Reverse Dictionary,* a much smaller and more idiosyncratic volume than the others, listed eighteen window-related words, but none of them was conceivably the one I wanted.

As for *underbelly,* the *Firefly* dictionary told me that *abdomen* was the word for that part of a bird, whereas the *Ultimate* dictionary call the part a *belly.* The *Illustrated Reverse Dictionary* contained a diagram of a bird with the relevant part labeled *belly.* I couldn't find any answer to the question in either the *Word Menu* or *Bernstein's.*

I should note that when I typed *"window parts"* and *"bird anatomy"* into the Google window on my computer, I was easily able to locate diagrams on the Internet that answered my questions (though the answer to the *mantel* question, according to a site called "How Your House Works," is *head jamb*).

In the end, I reached these conclusions:

- If you sometimes need a crash course in the terminology of a specific field—like basic astronomy or human anatomy or Gothic architecture—visual dictionaries can be a godsend.

- For obvious reasons, the terms given in visual dictionaries are invariably concrete. So if often the words you find yourself groping after are adjectives, verbs, and abstract nouns, the *Illustrated Reverse Dictionary* or the *Word Menu* will better serve your purposes.

Any of these books might well captivate a word lover—at least a word lover who isn't in a hurry. As you know, I'm a huge fan of

H. W. Fowler's *Modern English Usage,* but that's because I've taken the time to get acquainted with it. Anyone whose first exposure to Fowler comes when she or he is looking for a quick answer to a specific usage question is likely to come away frustrated and unenlightened. Similarly, visual and reverse dictionaries contain riches, but it's the person who spends some time with these books who is most likely to get their full benefit.

Tools for Detail Work

When I think about the next tool for finding just the right word, I remember a proud moment in my editing career. It began unpromisingly. I had done a lot of work on a 2,500-word magazine article and was showing the result to the writer, a swaggering and not very detail-oriented guy. He seized on one word in the edited copy and started giving me a hard time about it. His gist was that the word had a "feminine" quality and he would never have chosen it—so what *was* the word he'd used, and couldn't we go back to that? But he was wrong. I showed him the word in his original manuscript. He became sheepish and stopped complaining.

I'd spent a good deal of time hunting for just the right language to express what I thought he wanted to say, and I was proud to have succeeded well enough that he couldn't tell my work from his. (*I* could, though! I fixed his grammar, untangled his knotted sentences, and redirected toward their intended goal ones that had gone wandering off.) To get the job done, I made liberal use of my thesauri. (That's right, *thesauri.* That's the plural given first in all seven of our contemporary American dictionaries except the *Random House Webster's Unabridged.*) Thesauri and similar references are essential tools for writers, editors, and other word lovers, because they help us find words that maybe we wouldn't have thought of by ourselves.

New electronic resources as well as tried-and-true books exist, so recently I decided to see which of my options helped me the most, and which helped fastest. (Do those of us who use Microsoft Word need anything besides the thesaurus we can access by typing Shift F7?) I saved up a dozen sentences containing words or phrases I thought could be improved on—all from this chapter and the preceding one—and experimented with seven resources, which I've listed in the order of what I came to think of as roughly least to most helpful.

The back-cover copy of the *Random House Webster's Word Menu* calls it "a reverse dictionary, thesaurus, almanac, and compendious glossary all in one." As we saw earlier in this chapter, the *Word Menu* has its uses. But, alas, though it defines most of the not-quite-right words that came to my mind, it doesn't group them with words that are closely similar. For instance, *swaggering,* in the first paragraph of this section, is ruder than is fair to the person in question, but if you look up *swagger* in the *Word Menu,* you find the verb listed alphabetically among other "gaits" under "verbs of motion": *strut, stumble, stump, swagger, tiptoe . . . Swaggering* as an adjective, and *swagger* in any nonphysical sense, don't appear in the index at all. This book will help you focus a vague idea rather than perfect one that's just slightly off. It didn't help me with any of my twelve test sentences.

It is important to have an up-to-date dictionary and stylebook, I'm convinced, but I don't necessarily feel that way about other reference books. I dearly love my father's 1942 copy of *Webster's Dictionary of Synonyms,* because it's full of sturdy words that have withstood the test of time. Even the most recent edition of this book (titled *Merriam-Webster's Dictionary of Synonyms*) is time-tested, having been published in 1984. Dictionaries of synonyms are concerned with distinguishing between closely similar words, however, so the problem I had with this book was the opposite of the one I had with the *Word Menu:* it gave me a very short list of very close synonyms, and mostly I wanted ones further afield. *Webster's Dictionary of Synonyms* supplied workable solutions to just two of my twelve problems.

A mesmerizing electronic reference is the *Plumb Design Visual Thesaurus,* which comes in two editions: one that you can pay to install on your computer and a more basic one available online free. You can find both at www.visualthesaurus.com. I was disappointed that *Plumb* (I used the free edition) solved only four of my problems. In one instance, though, it was the only source that turned up anything I liked. For the phrase "contrary to his reputation as a defender of traditional distinctions" (which I wrote about Fowler in Chapter Six), I was looking for something less emphatic to substitute for *contrary to,* and within a few mouse clicks *Plumb* found me *out of keeping.* This little triumph was marred by a typo: the suggestion that *Plumb* actually presented me with was *out or keeping.* Oh, well.

In my little thesaurus competition, there was a tie for second place, between the Shift F7 thesaurus that is part of Microsoft Word and the electronic *Merriam-Webster's Collegiate Thesaurus,* which is included on the CD-ROM that comes with *Merriam-Webster's Collegiate Dictionary.* Each of these solved six of my problems (and not the same ones). This was just one less than the number of solutions—seven—I found in the sources that took first place. Here, also, there was a tie, between my father's 1942 copy of *Roget's Thesaurus* and *The Synonym Finder,* by J. I. Rodale, revised edition (1979).

I like my old *Roget's* for much the same reason as I like my old dictionary of synonyms: it's full of dignified, traditional words and phrases. And I got a kick out of using it in this test, because it supplied me with more vocabulary-building word trivia than any other source. I'd forgotten that *captious* means something like *contrary*—though that's *contrary* in the sense of "fault-finding," rather than "opposite." And how about *proficuous* as a synonym for *valuable* in the sense of "worthwhile," rather than "costly"? Obviously, neither of these words would be . . . um, a proficuous substitute for what I was seeking to replace. But *Roget's* also had plenty of down-to-earth ideas, such as *bluff* or *blustering* to replace *swaggering.* Ultimately, though, I decided that *bluff* alone was too cryptic and abrupt; *blustering* was just as rude as *swaggering;* and *bluff and blustering* was wordy—so I stuck with *swaggering* after all.

I've long been a fan of *The Synonym Finder,* so I wasn't surprised that it did well here. Whereas Peter Mark Roget, whose mid-nineteenth-century system of word classification underlies most of today's thesauri, had lofty philological and intellectual goals for his project, J. I. Rodale tried more straightforwardly, in the mid-twentieth century, to develop something that writers and editors needed. As the introduction to the first (1961) edition of this book says, "We have compiled many more synonyms than contained [*sic*] in any other book, and have placed them in the one place where they belong—under the word that is being looked up." The current edition is still more comprehensive and is organized in the same sensible way.

Why do I keep being taken aback when none of my resources does every last thing I want? Silly me. Here none of my resources was able to help me much more than half the time. I suppose if I'd had just one—almost any one of them—and had kept searching and searching, eventually I would have gotten somewhere. But my failures taught me lessons about how to make good use of synonym-finding tools:

- Forget about looking up most adverbs and participles, and look up the related adjectives and verbs instead. The second sentence of this section originally ended with *inauspiciously*—but that word was a little too fancy and fraught with superstition, I felt. Most of my resources in fact guided me toward *inauspicious* as the word to look up, and from there three sources suggested *unpromising*. It was easy enough to fill in the *-ly* ending myself. Similarly, most resources offered me many more possibilities for *swagger* (including ones that had to do with nonphysical senses of the word) than for *swaggering*.

- Try to think of *one* word close in meaning to what you're looking for, even if you're starting with a phrase that is still closer in meaning. My resources were least helpful when I wanted a synonym for more than one word: *contrary to,* for instance. *Plumb* came through with *out of keeping,* but all the other sources' suggestions, like *captious,* meant, simply, *contrary.*

- Stand ready to recast the sentence if you find a good word that doesn't fit the sentence you have. One of my test phrases was *injecting his own opinions,* and though I looked up *inject, opinion,* and *opine,* nothing suitable turned up except, from Word, *infuse. Infusing* [the book] *with his own opinions* isn't a bad way to say it. But ultimately I further revised the sentence, in Chapter Six, and ended up with "supplanting Fowler's point of view with his own."

- Before you settle on a word that you're not thoroughly famil-iar with, look it up in a dictionary to make sure it's as good a fit as you think it is. For example, under *largeness* or *size* or *immensity* several of the resources I've named give *enormity.* Nice word, huh? But according to all the more prescriptive stylebooks and usage manuals, *enormity* means "monstrous wickedness" or at least "the quality or state of being dreadful and overwhelming."

- Don't expect any one source to solve all your problems. Try out a range of sources and see which ones suit *you* best.

If you're surprised that anyone would go to all this trouble to get the words exactly right—well, of course you're not, or you wouldn't have read this far.

Talking Books

As long as we're being finicky (for a change!), let's be finicky about how to pronounce words too. As we discussed in Chapter Two, rarely do dictionaries look you in the eye and say "Pronounce it *this* way" unless there's really no question about how Americans (at least) pronounce the word. Again, where your dictionary gives al-ternatives, no one can tell you you're wrong if you simply go with the first pronunciation given. But, again, by putting a pronuncia-tion first, the dictionary's makers aren't indicating that they con-sider that pronunciation better (however they would construe that) or even necessarily more common than the other pronunciation or pronunciations given. If you want a firmer guide, you may wish to turn to *Garner's Modern American Usage,* by Bryan A. Garner, or to

The Big Book of Beastly Mispronunciations, by Charles Harrington Elster. Both are wide-ranging, contemporary, American, and scholarly. I don't agree with everything in either of them, but I'm always glad to know what the authorities who wrote these books think.

Remember the spelling and pronunciation question about *ambiance* versus *ambience,* which we asked in Chapter Two? And the pronunciation question about *Caribbean*? On the first of these, Garner says (I've taken slight liberties with his and Elster's orthography, for the sake of consistency and simplicity):

ambience; ambiance. These words denote the atmosphere of a place. *Ambience* (/am-bee-ən[t]s/) is an anglicized form that entered the language in the late 19th century. It's preferable to *ambiance* (/ahm-bee-ahn[t]s/), a Frenchified affectation that, since its proliferation in the mid-20th century, has become a vogue word. In modern print sources, *ambience* is used about three times as often as *ambiance.*

And Elster says:

ambience (or *ambiance*) *am*-bee-ints, not *ahm*-bee-ahnts. I prefer the spelling *ambience,* though it is less commonly used, because it better reflects the anglicized pronunciation recommended above.

Where Garner and Elster agree with each other, it's unsurprising. Elster served as a consultant on *Garner's Modern American Usage,* and Garner, in conversation, will readily tell you he has great respect for Elster's views on pronunciation. Where they differ, above, as to which spelling is more common, the disparity probably occurs because Elster has relied more heavily on reference books, such as dictionaries; and three of the more prescriptive dictionaries—the *AHD, Encarta,* and the *Random House Webster's Unabridged*—continue to treat *ambiance* as standard and *ambience* as a variant. Garner has used the Westlaw database to get firsthand information on "modern print sources."

Try checking edited-media sources yourself on Google News and you'll probably find a less dramatic gap between the incidence of *ambience* and *ambiance* than Garner found. When I looked, Google News pulled up 263 *ambience*s and 346 *ambiance*s from U.S. sources in the past month—hmm. However, Nexis reported 616 instances of *ambience* and 316 of *ambiance* in a month's worth of the two words in U.S. newspapers and newswires—more like a ratio of two to one than Garner's three to one, but still supporting his overall point.

As for *Caribbean,* the two authorities are both in favor of the pronunciation "kar-i-*bee*-ən." Garner says that pronunciation "is preferred because of its derivation from *Carib* /*kar*-ib/, the name of the native inhabitants of the islands that Christopher Columbus landed on and explored in 1493. . . ." And Elster gives a few reasons:

The evidence of my ears tells me this is still the prevailing pronunciation in the U.S. today, at least among the non–jet set. . . . [I]t is probably the dominant pronunciation in the Caribbean itself. . . . [and] despite more than sixty years of use in educated speech, kuh-*rib*-ee-in, wherever it came from, still retains a mysterious aroma of oily pseudosophistication.

Enough said!

❖

"Am I completely alone in pronouncing *often* with a silent *t*? Is that now deader than a doornail?"

My *Webster's Second Unabridged* (an edition published in the 1950s) notes that "until recently" pronouncing the *t* was often "considered as more or less illiterate" but that the educated "in some sections" do it. My *AHD* gives pronunciations with a *t* as the third and fourth among four choices and says in a usage note, "With the rise of public education and literacy and, consequently, people's awareness of spelling in the 19th century, sounds that had become silent sometimes were restored, as is the case with the *t* in often, which is now frequently pronounced." I don't suppose we can call pronouncing the *t* incorrect, then, though I agree with you that it's not ideal.

On this subject, Garner says, "The educated pronunciation is /*of*-ən/, but the less adept say /*of*-tən/." And Elster says flat out, "Do not pronounce the *t*," and then explains the convoluted history of the pronunciation of this word.

"Should not the word *culinary* be pronounced 'kyoo-li-nary,' with a long *u*? This is what my dictionary says and how I have always pronounced it, but for quite a while now I have been hearing everybody on the radio and TV cooking shows pronouncing it 'kull-i-nary.' At first I thought it was just a few mistaken people, but now it seems ubiquitous."

The unabridged *Webster's Third,* published in 1961, gave both pronunciations. That dictionary was firm in its intention to describe contemporary language, rather than prescribe how words ought to be used and pronounced—so the short *u* isn't something foisted on us by today's trendy foodies. The more prescriptive *AHD* still treats "kyoolinary" as the more common pronunciation, but there's no consensus.

Garner prefers "*kyoo*-le-ner-ee" but doesn't explain why. Elster says the word "properly" begins with *kyoo-*, though he admits it is "now usually" pronounced *kuhl-;* and he explains what a range of authorities have had to say about this word.

❖

"May I ask for clarification on the pronunciation of the term *short-lived*—specifically the latter part: *-lived.* It seems to be most often pronounced with a short *i,* as in 'Once, I *lived* in New York.' I am more comfortable with the long *i,* as in '*Live!* from New York!' My dictionary allows for both pronunciations. Why is it not simply spelled *short-lifed* and pronounced thus: 'My vacation in New York was *short-lifed,* because I was *knifed* in the back'? Friends and acquaintances—even my wife—seem compelled to correct me. Which of us is right?"

The word is etymologically nearer to the noun *life* than to the participle *lived,* and people who know that tend to pronounce it as you do, with the long *i.* So why isn't it *short-lifed*? If it had been coined yesterday, it probably would be. Time was, though, when the boundaries between *v* (or *u*) and *f* were more fluid than they are today. For instance, an antique form of your verb *knife* is *knive,* and a verb *wive* has existed for well over a millennium. As for *short-lived,* four hundred or so years ago it tended to appear as *short liu'd.* But the basic term has been in use that long—since the days of Shakespeare and Ben Jonson.

Hence, incidentally, it has far outlasted its ability to describe itself.

Garner (under *long-lived*) says: "The traditional AmE preference . . . has been to pronounce the second syllable /lɪvd/, not /livd/. . . . But the predominant practice today—and the BrE preference—is /livd/." Elster (also under *long-lived*) argues, on grounds of etymology and tradition, in favor of "lawng-lyvd," and gives no quarter to the short-*i* pronunciation.

❖

"I was recently looking up the word *Monday* in the dictionary with my third-grade students, and we made an amazing discovery. The preferred pronunciation of *Monday* is 'mun-dee,' with a long-*e* sound, not 'mun-day,' with a long-*a* sound. I checked other days of the week, and they were all the same: 'sun-dee' and so on. I checked other dictionaries and found the same thing. This doesn't sound right to me. Can you please explain?"

Dictionaries do tend to give both pronunciations, and some newish ones, such as *Encarta* and the *New Oxford American*, both from 1999, even put "mun-day" first. As for the long reign of "mun-dee," another correspondent of mine, an emeritus professor of English, knows a great deal more firsthand about this than I do, so I will let him explain: "All my old teachers, from the first grade through my doctorate, and my former-schoolmistress mother before them, insisted that the only acceptable pronunciation of the last syllable in the names of the days of the week was an unstressed '-dy,' as in *candy* and *handy*—that to sound it like the 'day' in *payday* or *May Day* was a 'spelling pronunciation' used by the imperfectly literate. But that was well over half a century ago, between World War I and

World War II. Today it is impossible to turn on the TV or radio without hearing some journalist speak of events happening 'mun-day' or 'thurs-day.'"

Garner discusses this issue only in passing, under *Wednesday*, which he says "is pronounced /*wenz*-day/ or /*wenz*-dee/." Elster calls "-day" a "so-called spelling pronunciation" but says he prefers it, and he explains that authorities (both in America and in Britain) have been arguing for some two hundred years about which pronunciation is dialect and which is standard.

"My mother, who majored in English in college, pronounced the word *sorbet* '*sor*-bet,' and so did I until a waiter, rather rudely, informed me that yes, the raspberry 'sor-*bay*' was available. Since that time I have found that almost everyone, including a TV advertiser, says 'sor-*bay*.' My *Merriam-Webster's Collegiate Dictionary,* ninth edition, however, tells me that the correct pronunciation is '*sor*-bet' and the word, like *sherbet,* is of Turkish origin. Would you comment?"

Gladly. The successors to your dictionary, the tenth and eleventh editions, have switched over to giving the "sor-*bay*" pronunciation first. This change amounts to Merriam-Webster's having revised its opinion about which pronunciation is more usual. Nonetheless, some other recent American dictionaries continue to favor "*sor*-bet." I confess that I can't recall ever hearing anyone pronounce the word this way, and I was first served sorbet many years ago, in a fancy French restaurant: the waiter presented each of us at the table with a dollop of very sweet fruit-flavored ice as a "palate cleanser" between the appetizer and the main course. Not until much later did I learn that sorbets intended to cleanse the palate needn't be sugary and French waiters needn't be pretentious.

In that long-ago waiter's defense, let it be said that although the word is indeed of Turkish origin, *sherbet* is the word that is thought to have come to us more or less directly from Turkish, whereas *sorbet* seems to have arrived in English by way of first Italian and then French. Nonetheless, I think I am going to start pronouncing the word "*sor*-bet." Now that you've made me aware of this pronunciation, I find its straightforwardly anglophone sound refreshing—almost as if the word itself were a palate cleanser.

Neither Garner nor Elster has anything to say about this one. But perhaps we've reviewed enough examples that we're ready to generalize:

- Because English is not a phonetic language, a person who invariably trusts "spelling pronunciations" is sometimes going to end up sounding foolish. (In fact, in the *other* column, Word Fugitives, that I write for *The Atlantic Monthly,* I once published this query from a reader: "Is there a word to describe someone who can read but can't pronounce words? One such person I know, who learned English from books, says things like 'Follow the gweed at the cathedral.'" Other readers then submitted hundreds of possible new terms to meet the need. The one I liked best was *tome-deaf.*) You're just not going to get *antipodes* or *chimera* or any of a number of other words right unless you've heard it said or studied up.

- In pronunciation, as in other aspects of English, tradition counts for a lot. But speech may be still more democratic than written English; how "everybody" now says a word counts even more. Before long, it may be time to throw in the kitchen towel on "kyoolinary." We each have to decide for ourselves how to weigh tradition against currency.

- Virtually all our vocabulary has been borrowed from people who pronounced the words differently than we do—whether the words come from Anglo-Saxon or Greek or Latin or French or Japanese. If a word or expression remains conspicuously borrowed without having yet been naturalized—for instance, *pfefferkuchen*—there's good reason to pronounce it in a foreign-sounding way. But once we English-speakers begin to think of the word as ours, too, we tend to make it conform to American English phonemes. In English, it tends to strike people as affected if you insist on pronouncing, oh, say, *chocolatier* as a French-speaker would when asking the concierge at a Parisian hotel where to find a good one.

A Few More Favorites

If you're a glutton for grammar and eager to learn more about it, have a look at *The Bedford Handbook* and *A Writer's Reference,* by Diana Hacker. *The Bedford Handbook,* bless it, is available on CD-ROM as well as in print.

Another kind of reference book that fascinates me, though I don't have much call to use it in my work, is the learners' dictionary. Learners' dictionaries tell you all sorts of things that are beneath the notice of regular dictionaries but that, even if you speak English with aplomb, can be worth reflecting on. For instance, in the well-regarded *Longman Dictionary of Contemporary English* (which comes with a CD-ROM), the entry for *car* not only defines the word ("a vehicle with four wheels and an engine, that can carry a small number of passengers") and tells you how to pronounce it, but also flags *car* as one of the 3,000 English words most commonly used; lists everyday phrases that include *car* ("by car, . . . drive a car, park a car, parked car, take the car [= drive it somewhere], car crash/accident . . . "); gives example sentences with *car*, many drawn from books and magazines; and, as a usage note, issues this injunction: "Do not use go in/out with 'car.' Use get in/out: *She got into her car (NOT went into her car) and drove off.* | *'Stop the car. I want to get out!' (NOT go out)*." By explaining things we know but perhaps did not realize we do, books like this can remind us how rich and deeply mysterious our language is.

Now I will gesture toward my biographical dictionary, an up-to-date atlas, two thirds of a shelf of foreign dictionaries (though pretty good translation resources are now easy to find online), and untidy heaps of historical works. (I don't get rid of old dictionaries, but I'm glad there are people who do: I *love* used-book stores.) And thus ends the tour of the major components of my language-reference library.

CHAPTER EIGHT

Do It Yourself

Remember "Should the *a* in *anthrax* be capped?" from Chapter Two? Getting that kind of thing right matters—at least when you're in public—but it's not intellectually stimulating. You open the dictionary or maybe type the word into the Google News window, you have your answer, and that's that. Language questions that reasonable people—including well-informed professional lexicographers, stylebook editors, and usage authorities—can and do disagree on are so much more exciting. And these questions come up all the time, as we've seen.

Granted, most people with language questions aren't asking them for the sheer joy of asking. They want answers, rather the way people who are pushing carts in a grocery store want to buy something to eat. But you and I are connoisseurs now. Look: the store is having a special on fresh duck breast—yum! That would be nice with a green-peppercorn sauce, don't you think? And, let's see, what would go well with it? In this warm weather, an arugula salad and some cornbread might be all we want—or wild rice can be really delicious . . .

Finding or, if need be, inventing solutions to people's language problems can be just as exhilarating as concocting a good meal. Some aspects of either process are well accepted: There is no point in marinating hamburger, because instead you can just mix a bit of the marinade into the chopped meat. There is no point in inventing new spellings for standard words. But many, many other aspects allow for—even demand—discretion and taste. Green-peppercorn sauce or à l'orange? Cornbread or wild rice? What's your pleasure?

Initially I divided the contents of this chapter into four sections: Questions with definitive answers that the people asking the questions just plain refuse to accept. Questions with definitive answers that are tricky to discover. "Damned if you do, damned if you don't" questions that clever people evade instead of answering. And questions to which there aren't definitive answers, giving us the opportunity to decide for ourselves.

But then I thought, What's intellectually stimulating about organizing the chapter that way? Let's mix the categories up. If you like, after you read any of the questions that follow, you can pause to decide which kind of question it is, consider how you'd go about answering it, and then compare that with what I say.

Acronyms, possessives of

See *Possessives of initialisms and acronyms*.

Allegator, Alleger

"Whenever I hear a news report about an allegation that's been made, I wonder whether the person making it should be referred to as an *alleger* or as an *allegator.* A person who drives is a *driver,* but one who conserves is a *conservator,* so there does not seem to be a clear rule. If *allegator* is chosen, the question of pronunciation will arise: should it be 'allege-ator,' as the origin of the word suggests, or 'alle-gator,' which defendants and lawyers would probably prefer?"

According to *Webster's Third* and the *Oxford English Dictionary,* both words exist. *Alleger* is more common, though, and *allegator* doesn't seem to be gaining on it. (The *OED* labels *allegator* "obsolete,"* and when it does turn up in print citations nowadays, it is more often than not a typo for *alligator.*) *Allegator* joined the language together with *allegation,* as *conservator* did with *conservation.* The problem with it is exactly that it is pronounced like the fellow with the jaws and the sharp teeth. May I render a snap judgment? Go with *alleger.*

Alumnae, Alumni, Alumni/ae

"My colleagues and I in a university alumni publications office regularly have heated debates over the use of the words related to *alumni.* Urged on by frequent comments from our readers, we have been sticking by our Latin grammar books. Our style guide says: '*Alumni* and *alumnae, alumni/ae:* Do not use *alumni* to include both male and female graduates except in proper names such as the *University Business School Alumni Association.* Use either of the preceding phrases (*alumni and alumnae, alumni/ae*) but, for aesthetic reasons, do not use *alumni/ae* excessively. When referring to a graduate or group of graduates of a single gender, be specific: *one alumnus* or *two alumni* (male); *alumna* or *alumnae* (female).'

"Our latest debate began when a reader wrote in to argue that *alumni* is plural but without gender and so can be used to refer to a group. In revisiting this in *Merriam-Webster's Collegiate,* our reference dictionary, I find that *alumni* indeed has no gender attached. Is it safe to change our style guide?"

According to my Latin resources, if you want to be true to the words' origins, you'll keep following your style guide. There is no such thing as a gender-neutral noun in Latin—or, rather, every Latin noun is masculine, feminine, or neuter, with "neuter" being comparable to *it,* not to *he/she.* When the Latin word is being used as a subject, *alumnus* and *alumni* are the masculine forms, you know what the feminine forms are, and *alumnum* and *alumna* (a plural that's the same as the feminine singular and is therefore likely to flummox most English-speakers) are the neuter forms.

Latin conventionally uses the masculine plural for mixed-sex groups, somewhat the way English traditionally used *he* and other masculine singular forms to mean "anyone." I'd imagine this is what your argumentative reader has in mind. But that's exactly what younger people—especially younger female ones—object to. So I wish I could tell you that *alumni* is neutral, but it's not. Alas, I can't even advise you to switch to *graduates,* since, as I'm sure you know, a person need not graduate from a school but only attend it to be considered an alum.

Anathema

"Dictionaries say that *anathema* is a singular noun (plural *anathemas*). I wonder why writers often tend to drop the article or treat the singular as plural: 'Clichés, the "coin(s) so battered by use as to be defaced," are *anathema* to Partridge.' This usage seems to fly in the face of the definition. Is it simply a case of misuse, or is there more to it? I have searched stylebooks, reference materials, and Web sites, but I find nothing about this particular issue."

Not all singular nouns are heralded by articles: think of *anxiety* or *beauty.* But one would expect *anathema,* which means approximately "a loathsome or accursed thing," to take an article, the way "loathsome thing" does. If you want to know whether *anathema* behaves as expected, the quickest way to find out is to type *anathema* into the Google News window and count how many of *an anathema* and how many of *anathema* alone you get. I just tried this, and of the first fifty results, only four—three of which were from non-U.S. sources—used the article *an. Anathema* alone is clearly the norm.

As for why that's the case, no doubt it has something to do with the word's history. The *OED* gives this definition (among others): "Anything accursed, or consigned to damnation. Also quasi-*adj.* Accursed, consigned to perdition." Citations under that definition, from 1634 and 1765 respectively, read, "Delivered over unto Satan, proclaimed publicans, heathens, *anathema,*" and "Saint Paul wished to become *anathema* himself, so he could thereby save his brethren." Which says to me that we have an established, if unusual, idiom here. And the note calling the word a quasi-adjective that means "accursed" is another hint that no article need be used with *anathema.* Shall we leave it at that?

Anniversary

"Another anniversary of the attack on the World Trade Center towers and the Pentagon is fast approaching as I write this: When was the last time you heard or read the word *anniversary* not preceded by a hyphenated modifier relating the length of time being noted or celebrated? Other than among a small coterie of sensible friends, I am beginning to have difficulty remembering when people said *second anniversary* rather than *two-year anniversary*. Then there is that totally illogical phrase *two-month anniversary*. Is there a chance this is merely a fad that will pass? Or are we going to be stuck with it?"

> You are, of course, alluding to the fact that the *anni-* in *anniversary* means "year," so *two-year anniversary* is redundant and *two-month anniversary* is a mishmash. As I write this, an anniversary of the terrorist attacks is recently past, so I searched Nexis's U.S. news sources from September 11, 2003, for you. On that day alone more than 150 instances of *year anniversary* were published. Numerous mainstream sources, like the AP and *USA Today*, were guilty of the solecism. On the same day, however, more than five times as many articles using the phrase *second anniversary* appeared; the AP and *USA Today* were well represented in this group, too. So "sensible" people are in the majority after all.
>
> The *two-month anniversary* problem is more complicated, because no word or set phrase is available to do the job, so rephrasing is generally required. We might, for instance, change "the newlyweds celebrated their *two-month anniversary*" to ". . . celebrated having been married two months."

I hope you don't think my responses to the last two questions amount to "If most people say something a certain way, that's the right way to say it." What most people say is certainly worth knowing; it's a factor. To my mind, though, an equally important factor is tradition: Have most people been saying the thing in question for a long time? The reason this matters to me is not that I prefer the past to the future. Traditional language is durable language. Yet another factor is the word's derivation: When you hear or read a word, what does it tell you about itself? To me, the relationship between the *anni-* part of *anniversary* and *annual* and *per annum* and *anno Domini,* or A.D., is too close to ignore. Even if everybody now did say *two-year anniversary,* I . . . Well, but not everyone does say that, and those who do say it generally reform once they realize that *anni-* means "year." Derivation, along with tradition, matters to many of us.

Anti-Semite

"According to my dictionary, an Arab is a *Semite.* The editors of the newspaper *The Oregonian* keep saying that the Arab terrorists are *anti-Semitic.* It would seem to me that the Arabs may be *anti-Jew* or *anti-Israel,* but since they are *Semites,* they can hardly be considered *anti-Semites.* When did the word *anti-Semite* come to mean 'anti-Jew'? Does *anti-Semite* now mean only 'anti-Jew'?"

You're right that the *Semitic* peoples include Arabs as well as Jews. But according to the *OED,* ever since the words *anti-Semite, anti-Semitic,* and *anti-Semitism* began to appear in print, in the 1880s, they have had to do with hostility or opposition to Jews and only Jews. As for why that's the case, I fear this is one of the many questions about English that can be much more readily asked than answered.

Artwork

"I am being driven crazy by the ubiquitous use of the term *artwork.* I first encountered this term in the 1970s, in the context of 'camera-ready artwork' for a party invitation. Now the *Mona Lisa* is *artwork*, the Sistine Chapel ceiling is *artwork*, and both are treated linguistically as though they were on the same level artistically as my invitation. What is wrong with the word *art*, and why is *artwork* replacing it?"

More and more often one does see citations like the following, from an article that appeared in *USA Today* about the former Tyco CEO Dennis Kozlowski: " . . . \$13 million of old masters and impressionist *artwork*." You're right, too, that *artwork* in its traditional, standard meaning is a good deal less high-toned than *art* can be. It's either a printing term, as you note, or descriptive of "artistic" things "produced in quantity," according to a definition in *Webster's Third*.

Because many people would rather not use three words where one will do, the extended sense has come about (or so I suspect) owing to the likes of this: "The *Mona Lisa* is among Western civilization's most familiar . . ." Tradition calls for the thought to be completed with *works of art*, but some people would naturally assume that *artworks* is an equivalent term. It isn't, quite. And certainly where *art* by itself passes muster (as it would have in the *USA Today* citation), it is preferable.

Attorney general

See *General*.

Biannual, Biennial

See *Three times a year*.

Bred

"I wonder if anyone has ever asked you to discuss the rather unfortunate use of the word *bred*. For example, I recently read on a novel's jacket that the author had been born and *bred* in North Carolina. I am aware that one of the meanings of this word is 'raised' or 'nurtured.' However, every time I have encountered this usage, it is within the context of describing a woman's background, never a man's, so I can't shake the initial connotation that comes to my mind: that the woman was literally *bred,* as if she were a heifer. Maybe you can shed some light on how this use of this word evolved and then perhaps conjure up a reason for its persistence."

Will you feel better to learn that the word is not only, or even primarily, applied to females? The week before I wrote this, *The Orlando Sentinel* called a male filmmaker "Brooklyn-born, Queens-*bred,*" the *Los Angeles Times* called an all-male quintet "Los Angeles-based, Omaha-*bred,*" and *The Village Voice* referred to a legal case as having "*bred* numerous law-review essays."

What's more, if you're going to reject as unseemly any word that can possibly have a whiff of the barnyard about it—well, there go *have* and *take* and *cover* and *reproduction* and *stud earrings* and heaven only knows what else. *Bred* is just a derivative of the verb *breed*. According to the *OED,* a thousand-year-old meaning of this verb is "Said of a female parent: To cherish (brood) in the womb or egg; to bring (offspring) forward from the germ to the birth; to hatch (young birds) from the egg; to produce (offspring, children)." Several centuries old is the meaning "to train up to a state of physical or mental development"; the *OED* explains that this sense was "evidently transferred" from the meaning just cited, "the young creature being viewed as a rude germ to be developed by nurture." A supporting citation from 1570 reads, "One of the best Scholers that euer S. Johns Colledge *bred.*" A reason, then, to continue using *bred* with the meaning "brought up" or "trained" is that well-bred people have been using it that way for many generations.

Crisp, Crispy

"Would you please discuss the adjectives *crisp* and *crispy*? I'm not satisfied with the dictionary treatment of them. Do we need *crispy*? If we don't need it, why does it persist? Could it be that the trochaic *crispy* fits more mellifluously into advertising jingles?"

Crispy certainly is persistent: it has been part of our language for at least six hundred years. Early on it meant "curled," as did *crisp.* Some reputable present-day dictionaries declare it to be no more and no less than a synonym for *crisp*—but who ever says "I admire her *crispy* efficiency" or "It was a *crispy* spring morning"? Nonphysical meanings don't apply to this word. Then again, I don't think many people would say that they like fried chicken best when it's *crisp*—and I don't mean they like it soggy. Fries and bacon, however, may be preferred either *crisp* or *crispy,* according to my databases. You're right that English doesn't really need *crispy,* but what do you say we keep it anyway, if only out of respect for tradition?

Entrée

"Growing up in Montreal, where French and English mingle more than they do in many places, I was accustomed to ordering an *en-*

trée before the main course, even on English-language menus. When I moved to the States, I found that the *entrées* in fact *were* the main course and that an *appetizer* whetted the palate. Now that I'm in London, I can't find *entrées* anywhere and have to be content with *starters*. Can you comment on the seemingly strange usage of *entrée* in the United States?"

Either some of my sources are mistaken or everyone has been waffling on the meaning of this word. In French, in non-culinary contexts, *entrée* of course means things like "entry" and "beginning," so it's unsurprising to find that the classic mid-nineteenth-century French dictionary *Littré* defined the culinary *entrée* as a dish served at the outset of a meal. However, by the mid-twentieth century *Webster's Second* was reporting that an *entrée* is "in French usage, a dish served between the chief courses." The same dictionary went on to say that "in English usage" the word refers to "a rather elaborate made dish served before the roast, such as creamed sweetbreads, a fruit fritter, or a timbale; also the course in which it is served," and that "in hotel usage" an *entrée* is "a meat dish not classed as a roast; also a meat substitute, such as macaroni and cheese." This last idea is probably where the now standard American sense, "the main course of a meal," came from, as most of us stopped demanding fish *and* an entrée *and* roasted meat, plus soup and dessert, on a typical evening. Indeed, by the mid-twentieth century other American dictionaries were giving "main course" as an alternative meaning for *entrée.*

The English *starter,* by the way, is an upstart. The *OED* calls it colloquial, and some of its citations, all dating from 1966 to 1979, are contemptuous: for instance, "There was avocado pear for what some people disgustingly called '*starters*.'" *Starter* has nonetheless begun to appear in American dictionaries as a synonym for *appetizer,* without any notation about its being either British or cheesy.

First-generation

"I have always thought that *first-generation American* referred to someone who was the first person in a family line to be born in the United States. But a friend insists that *first-generation American* may refer to someone who immigrates here and becomes a U.S. citizen. Who is right? Have I suddenly changed from a third-generation to a fourth-generation American?"

Dictionaries define, and newspaper and magazine citations use, the term both ways. Strangely enough, *first-generation* seems never to have had one unmistakable meaning. At least, the earliest dictionary entry I've been able to find, in *Webster's Third,* reads like this: "1: born in the U.S.—used of an American of immigrant parentage 2: foreign-born—used of a naturalized American." So the term is useless, I'm afraid, except where context clarifies which of its meanings is intended. And that's not much of an exception, because if other words make the point, why make it again?

Flammable, Inflammable

"For the past thirty-five years I have tossed and turned at night wondering why some gasoline tanker trucks have the warning *flammable* and some have the warning *inflammable.* The dictionary gives a similar definition for each. How about a little help so I can get a full night's sleep?

"P.S. My wife just reminded me that *valuable* and *invaluable* have the same meaning. The plot thickens!"

We're all familiar with pairs of antonyms like *ability* and *inability*, *authentic* and *inauthentic*—so pairs of synonyms constructed on the same pattern do seem like the result of poor planning. But the *OED* gives four entries for the prefix *in-*, only one of which carries the meaning "not." The other meanings of *in-* are illustrated by words like *include, income, inside, insight, insure,* and *intake,* in which the prefixes mostly signify variations on or extensions of the idea of "in" or "into." (Though the three prefixes mean roughly the same thing, the *OED* divides them up according to when and from where they arrived in English.)

Inflammable means that the gasoline or what have you can be *inflamed,* in that verb's oldest sense of being "set on fire" or "bursting into flames." Interestingly (by the way, the beginning of *interestingly* has an altogether different derivation), the prefix in *invaluable* is the one that means "not." "Above and beyond valuation" and "too great to be estimated" are among the *OED*'s definitions for this word.

For, Of

"I work in the technical editing department of a large software company. I'm having a friendly debate with a colleague about whether to use *for* or *of* in a particular context. Our house style guide has a section titled 'Spelling and Usage of Common Terms' and a subsection called 'Usage for Selected Terms.' I suggested to my colleague that we change the subsection title to 'Usage of' to agree with the other title. She feels that, yes, we should be consistent, but in both cases the word should be *for.* She prefers *for* because she hears the subsection title as meaning 'here are the usage guidelines *for* these terms.' My ear tells me *of.* Which of us is right?"

It's *usage of* a term, not *usage for* it, so I side with you. The problem with your colleague's argument is that it requires us all to hear the same implied word, *guidelines,* after *usage*—but that word isn't present, and *usage* is a perfectly good noun in its own right. Nonetheless, trying to find a form that sounds right to everyone never hurts. Maybe "Spelling and Usage Guidelines for Common Terms" and "Usage Guidelines for Selected Terms"?

Fraternal, Sororal

"Recently I became a grandfather of twin girls who are not identical. People have been referring to them as *fraternal* twins—but they're girls. I've been calling them *sororal.* What do you think?"

Makes sense to me. *Sororal* is indisputably a word meaning "sisterly"—a counterpart to *fraternal,* whose principal meaning is "brotherly." Although dictionaries tend to define *fraternal twin* as applying to members of both sexes, I can't imagine anyone misunderstanding you or, in these days of egalitarianism, reacting to your expression with anything but an appreciative chuckle.

Fundraiser, Fund-raiser

"The dictionary shows *fund-raiser* as a hyphenated word, but many nonprofit agencies are spelling it as one word without the hyphen.

Is this a word whose spelling has changed? I'm doing a brochure and I need to know!"

This is a word whose spelling is *changing,* toward the closed-up form. For now, though, there's no consensus. Three of the seven major American dictionaries either give only the closed-up form or prefer it; the other four give only or prefer the hyphenated form. The word is seen both ways (and also occasionally as *fund raiser*) in Nexis citations. If you're inclined to be progressive, embrace *fundraiser;* if you're more conservative, stick with *fund-raiser.*

General

"Here in Washington, D.C., I have observed the increased misuse of the title *General* in addressing the present Attorney General—as in '*General* Ashcroft.' I was a consul general for several years in three different countries but was never addressed as *General*. If '*General* Ashcroft' is correct, does it follow that we should so address the other civilian generals: Surgeon, Solicitor, Comptroller, Director, and so forth? Or should we reserve the title for military generals?"

You're right that John Ashcroft is sometimes called "*General* Ashcroft." For instance, the CNN television-show host Larry King referred to the Attorney General that way in September of 2003. You're right, too, that this usage is wrong.

In fact, even in military usage *general* was originally an adjective. Time was, that is, when *brigadier general* and *major general* were understood as terms parallel to *consul general* and *attorney general;* all these terms, as Steven Pinker notes in his book *Words and Rules*, "were borrowed from French when England was ruled by the Normans in the centuries after the invasion of William the Conqueror in 1066." In French most descriptive adjectives are used "postpositively," or after the noun, though this word order is relatively rare in English. Thus our military noun and military title arose through misunderstanding. By now they've won legitimacy— but only in military usage. Anyone in the U.S. Army, Air Force, or Marine Corps above the rank of colonel may properly be called *General,* but no civilian should be.

As soon as I published that, follow-up letters began arriving. For example:

"I must take issue with your pronouncement that the title *General* is never appropriate for a civilian. I served as an assistant attorney general in Tennessee and can tell you that it is long-standing tradition, indeed expected etiquette, to address the state attorney general and assistant attorneys general as *General* So-and-So. This is true in many southern states. In Tennessee it also applies to local prosecutors and their assistants, because their title is District Attorney General. Observe any criminal case there to confirm this.

"This is not just a southern quirk. I have confirmed through first-hand observers that in the United States Supreme Court, the justices commonly address the U.S. Attorney General, the U.S. Solicitor General, and state attorneys general by the title *General.* If good enough for the Supreme Court, then good enough for me.

"When I moved to Indiana and began serving as a deputy attorney general here, I learned that the tradition had not migrated northward. In fact, the attorneys general whom I have served are downright uncomfortable when addressed as *General.* I sure miss having judges address me as *General!*

"Whether or not *general* is an adjective, I believe this accepted usage has made it legitimate to address General Ashcroft as such."

And a communications specialist in the U.S. Army sent me this:

"Even in the military, we have the 'non-military' use of the word *general.* For example, it is perfectly accurate to say that most adjutants general are *major generals,* whereas most inspectors general are not *generals* at all."

Around the time these missives were arriving, I happened to talk with Bryan Garner and mentioned my readers' complaints. To cheer me up, he forwarded me an e-mail that he'd received after teaching a seminar at the Department of Justice:

"I enjoyed the class at DOJ, but I take issue with your reference to the attorney general as *General* Ashcroft. The attorney general is not a general; he is an attorney who does general legal work for the government. The word *general* is an adjective, not a noun. The plural of *attorney general* is *attorneys general.* The reporters who address the attorney general as '*General* Ashcroft' at press conferences are simply wrong. In all other respects, however, your presentation was excellent."

I give up. When you invite the Attorney General over for dinner, you're on your own as to how to introduce him to the other guests.

Gone missing

"I thought that you needed only a form of the verb *to be* to express the following: 'He *is missing*.' Lately, though, from various sources including newscasters, I have noticed the thought expressed somewhat differently: 'He's *gone missing*.' From where has this *gone missing* come? Isn't it redundant?"

He's gone missing conveys a different shade of meaning from either *He is missing* or *He is gone,* signifying something more like "He has disappeared." American dictionaries that give the phrase are likely to tell you it's "chiefly British." Nonetheless, it is indeed increasingly common in American English. I see no reason to object to it—but may I suggest that we draw the line at the nonsensical *turned up missing*? This turns up surprisingly often, and it comes predominantly from American sources.

Grill, Grille

See *Point, Pointe.*

Ice cream

"My brother and I are having a dispute about *ice cream.* I contend it is two words. It is listed that way in the dictionary, and if you were playing Scrabble, it would be challenged and you would be forced to take it from the board (or so says my Scrabble dictionary). My brother contends that it is one word, because if you were diagramming a sentence, *ice cream* would 'hold the place of' one word, not two. Your input on this would be appreciated."

It's true that the rules printed on the Scrabble box say:

Before the game begins, players should agree which dictionary they will use, in case of a challenge. All words labeled as a part of speech . . . are permitted with the exception of the following: words always capitalized, abbreviations, prefixes and suffixes standing alone, words requiring a hyphen or an apostrophe.

It's also true that all the major contemporary American dictionaries (except Scrabble dictionaries) have entries for *ice cream*, and these give "noun" as its part of speech. But is it a word? In defining *word*, the *Random House Webster's Unabridged Dictionary* says, "Words are usually separated by spaces in writing," and other dictionaries echo that idea.

Do linguists—scientists of words—agree? In fact they don't tend to use *word* to mean anything very precise, instead discussing the likes of *morphemes* and *listemes* and *syntactic atoms*. In the glossary of his book *The Language Instinct*, Steven Pinker explains this last term as "one of the senses of 'word,' defined as an entity that the rules of syntax cannot separate or rearrange." That seems to be the sense of *word* that your brother has in mind. He's right that *ice cream* is a word for some purposes. And you are right that it is not a word for Scrabble's purposes—though *amerce, macer,* and *racemic* (each of which uses only letters from *ice cream*) all pass muster. Go figure.

If

"Almost everyone has had the experience of looking at a word and finding that it suddenly no longer makes sense. I'm currently having a similar experience, consistently, with an entire verb form: the subjunctive. Put a sentence containing *if* and a form of *to be* in front of me and I'm in la-la land.

"Case in point: In the latest issue of your *Copy Editor* newsletter, I read, 'What would you do with this sentence if the reversal of the decision was what was in the news that day?' This doesn't sound wrong to me, but I can't help wondering why that first *was* isn't *were*. Or should I say 'wondering if that first *was* were not more correctly *were*'?"

There is no consensus on exactly where to use subjunctives, so you have good reason to be confused. As *Merriam-Webster's Dictionary of English Usage* explains:

Bernstein 1971 [*Miss Thistlebottom's Hobgoblins*] and Bryson 1984 [*Bryson's Dictionary of Troublesome Words,* a revised and updated edition of which was published in 2002] try to distinguish between uses of *if* where the subjunctive is called for and uses where it is to be avoided. Both allow the subjunctive after *if* when the clause contains a condition that is hypothetical or contrary to fact, but neither gives a satisfactory rule of thumb for identifying such clauses. The problem is that the dividing line between what is or could well be true and what is hypothetical or not true is not consistently clear—in fact it can often be an entirely subjective judgment made by the writer.

Case in point: Some time ago for *Copy Editor* I polled authorities by e-mail about how they'd render in print a spoken reference to September 11, 2001 (that is, how they thought "He said, '9/11 had a huge impact on our society'" should be written). Allan M. Siegal, a co-author of *The New York Times Manual,* wrote, "If '9/11' were unavoidable at the start of a sentence, I'd try to avoid it anyway, although if it were in a quotation, and the quotation were preceded by attribution, I'd have no objection to starting the quotation with the figures." At the last minute one of the newsletter's copy editors and I said to each other, Gosh, in Siegal's answer those *shouldn't* be subjunctives, should they?, because hypothetical though those situations may be, he's talking about real possibilities. So I changed both instances of *were* to *was* in his answer as it was published in *Copy Editor.* (I know, it was high-handed of me—but as I said, the question came up at the last minute.)

That elicited a follow-up e-mail from Siegal: "This is not a complaint, just a deep sigh. I'm quite sure that I indeed e-mailed 'if 9/11 was' and 'if it was' in my response to your question. If anyone asks, I'm abashed. Those should both be subjunctives." I replied, explaining what had happened and why. He wrote back to say that we differed on the rule, and quoted from his stylebook, which says about the subjunctive, "Use this form of verb to express a wishful notion or a proposition contrary to fact. . . . Do not use the subjunctive form (even with a tantalizing *if* in the sentence) when the intent is merely to convert an *is* idea to the past tense."

So in the sentence you quote, in my opinion the subjunctive is not called for, because what's under discussion, though hypothetical, is being presented as a real possibility: What *would* you do if that *was* the case? But this time I'm going to let Siegal have the last word. I e-mailed him about your question and he responded: "I'm feeling less dogmatic now than when I wrote to you. Researching the question afterward, I found your principle expressed in several authoritative reference works. I still side

with Bill Bryson, though: 'One small hint: if the sentence contains *would* or *wouldn't,* the mood is subjunctive, as in "If I were
you, I wouldn't take the job."' For an assembly-line copy desk
working under deadline pressure, that test is commendably
practical."

I let Siegal have the last word in the newsletter because fair's fair.
But what he said amounts to his agreeing to disagree with me. And
now that you know both sides of the argument, you can decide for
yourself what you think.

Increasingly more

"Lately I've noticed writers pairing the word *increasingly* with a
comparative adjective form—for example, *increasingly more popular* or *increasingly longer.* Isn't this construction redundant?
Wouldn't *increasingly popular, more popular, increasingly long,* or
longer suffice?"

When I got your e-mail, my first thought was that you had done
my job for me and all I'd need to do was say you were right. But
once I looked at a number of sentences in print that include *increasingly more,* I began to sympathize with a few of the writers
and their editors.

You *are* right that in the great majority of instances *increasingly*
followed by a comparative is bad form—a redundancy that can
easily be solved by changing the phrase to the likes of *increasingly
popular.* Occasionally, though, *more* is serving as a pronoun, and
then you may need to take unusual measures. Consider this sentence, from a recent trade-magazine article: "While the industry

focuses on audience ratings as a basic definition of value in media, we all know that there is *increasingly more* to this game than just whether eyeballs happen to be in the room when the television set is on." Here *increasingly* and *more* are doing different jobs. You could say, instead, "*increasingly,* there is *more* to this game than . . ." If that were my sentence, I think I would move the *increasingly* or else tuck a pair of commas around it. Although the construction is almost always redundant and wrong, this is a case in which it is not.

Surprisingly often, there are exceptions to even such seemingly obvious rules as "Don't write *increasingly more,* because it's redundant." When looking into questions like this, I find my online databases, Nexis and Google News, invaluable, because they show me real-world examples that I never would have dreamed up.

Initialisms, possessives of

See *Possessives of initialisms and acronyms.*

Inspires confusion

"My wife used the phrase *inspires confusion,* as in 'His music *inspires confusion* in listeners.' I said confusion is not normally a product of an inspirational experience. She said she was using *inspires* in a straightforward fashion, such usage being sanctioned by the eighth or ninth dictionary definition of *inspire,* which indeed suggests that *inspire* can mean nothing more than 'cause.' I replied that *sows* or *causes* is better. I pointed out that most definitions of *inspire* (such as 'exert an exalting influence' or 'impel') trade metaphorically on its derivation from *breathe* (albeit in a transitive sense—that is, to animate something by infusing it with vital air). I maintained that even if the metaphor is for the most part forgotten, it lurks just powerfully enough beneath the surface to sow confusion as to how something life-giving (a breath of air) can create something life-muddling (a state of confusion). Naturally, my wife thinks I'm a perfect ass. This may be true, but I'd like your opinion (well, support)."

It's easy to get carried away with niceties like this, and the language is rife with them. Does a dog have a *person*ality, for instance? Is *awfully cruel* redundant?

The living, breathing inspirational connotations of *inspire* would keep me, for one, from joining that word with *confusion*. And, in fact, the combination is unusual, turning up about as often in periodicals as the typo *carful* where *careful* belongs. But some of those few *inspire* (or *inspires*) *confusion* citations come from such reputable sources as *The Philadelphia Inquirer* and the *Los Angeles Times*. So I wouldn't say that your wife is wrong. It's a matter of taste.

Please don't assume, by the way, that the first dictionary definition for any given word is the primary one. Your dictionary's front matter will tell you whether its "eighth or ninth" definition of *inspire* is meant to be less prevalent or important than ones higher on the list.

Did I say I liked *inspires confusion*? But somebody's always got to be a critic.

"I am stunned that you cited the *Los Angeles Times* as a reputable source, thus justifying the internally contradictory *inspiring confu-*

sion. Simply because you saw it in print someplace does not mean it is correct. You would not believe the egregious misuses of words and phrases that I have caught the *Times* in, the most recent of which was *tact* for *tack.*

"Your misguided justification is about as bad as blessing *nucular* for *nuclear* because you heard the President say it and therefore it must be right. You can do better than that. *Inspiring confusion* simply doesn't work, no matter how hard you push it."

Kudo, Kudos

"I started to write you a slightly snippy letter because in an article you published recently, the author, Constance Hale, used the phrase 'half a kudo,' and as far as I knew, there is no such word as *kudo.* Traditionally *kudos* has been treated as a singular noun, transliterated from the Greek, meaning 'praise' or 'credit.'

"Then, on a hunch, I went to *Webster's Third,* and by golly it lists *kudos* as a plural noun—although it doesn't offer a singular form. I often disagree with *W3,* and this is an instance of such disagreement. But now I'm compelled to acknowledge that there is some official support for the plural construction. So instead of feeling snippy, I now just feel grumpy and slightly old.

"Any thoughts on this matter?"

Take another look at *Webster's Third.* If your copy says the same thing as mine (and there's a possibility it doesn't—lexicographers tinker with their dictionaries from one copyright printing to the next), it lists *kudos* as a noun, by which it means a singular noun, whose plural, it says, is also *kudos.*

I looked in the *OED,* too, where I was fascinated to see that *kudos* itself is labeled *"slang"* and *"colloquial."* As for *kudo,* the

OED calls it a singular back-formation resulting from erroneously treating *kudos* as a plural. Most language authorities join the *OED* in treating *kudo* as something people say or write out of ignorance. But I know perfectly well that *kudo* isn't a proper word. And because I'm acquainted with Connie Hale, I didn't doubt for an instant, when I saw it in her manuscript, that she also knew what was correct and preferred to be playful.

When is being strict about the rules in the best interests of the writer and readers, and when isn't it? I have no idea how many readers reacted as I did to "half a kudo," because readers rarely write letters about things like that. If I had this to do over again, though, I don't think I would plead with Hale to change her phrase, because I enjoyed it.

Latin America

"I've never heard anyone refer to the northern section of the Americas as *Anglo America.* So why do we keep using the term *Latin America*? Isn't it blatantly racist and inaccurate? I tried to think of other cases in which ethnicity is used to describe (in modern English) what is supposed to be a geographic location, but I couldn't find any."

In fact whole wide swaths of the world were long ago named after the people who had settled them. You're right that this hasn't happened much lately—though *the Slavic countries* may be another example. These terms aren't racist, only socially descriptive in a way that, say, *South America* is not. Puerto Rico and Guadeloupe, for example, are invariably considered *Latin;*

whether the term covers Belize and Guyana (on the mainland but English-speaking) is now a matter of debate. *Latin America* originally designated the southerly portion of the American continental landmass and the nearby islands where the primary official languages were derived from Latin. Just don't ask me why no one ever looked north and included Quebec.

Little

"'It's become painfully obvious how little organic beef, pork, and chicken is available in stores.' That's *is,* not *are,* correct? I know *little* is usually considered a singular indefinite pronoun, but *beef, pork, and chicken* throws me."

First let's get it straight that in your sentence *little* is not a pronoun. (Though it can be a noun, *little* is actually never a pronoun. Consider a sentence that the *RHUD* gives for the noun use: "If you want some ice cream, there's a *little* in the refrigerator." *Little* there is a noun, and never mind that if you replaced it and its article, *a,* with *some, some* would be a pronoun.) Rather, *little* is an adjective in your sentence, modifying *beef, pork, and chicken.*

Since three nouns are the subject of the clause, shouldn't the verb be plural? Not necessarily. I'd say you're using the three to express one concept: meat. And as *Garner's Modern American Usage* explains it, "If the subjects really amount to a single . . . thing, use a singular verb." You *would* want to say "The recipes I have for the main course and the dessert won't work because of how *little meat and chocolate are* available." In this new example, though, *meat* and *chocolate* are conceptually separate, and the idea expressed in full would be ". . . how little meat and how little chocolate are available." But in effect you are saying "how *little* organic *meat is* available," so the singular verb is fine.`

Log into, Log in to, Log onto, Log on to

"To direct readers to a Web site, we often use the phrase *log onto www.webaddress.com.* Which is correct: *onto* or *on to?*"

To get technical, what your question amounts to is whether you're using the verb *log* followed by the prepositional phrase *onto www.webaddress.com* or using the phrasal verb *log on* followed by the prepositional phrase *to www.webaddress.com.*

In Internet contexts *log* is almost invariably followed by *on* (or *in* or *off* or *out*); the two words together have a meaning distinct from that of the verb *log* alone; and they appear together as a phrasal verb in some of the more up-to-date dictionaries. If the choice is simply between the alternatives we started with, *log on to* is what you want.

To get technical in a different way, though, *log in to* and the noun *login* are still more common in Internet contexts. Google gave me these raw tallies of Web pages containing the various forms (I've listed them in order of ascending popularity):

Logon to = 263,000
Log onto = 494,000
Log into = 1,200,000
Log on to = 1,610,000
Login to = 4,310,000
Log in to = 4,610,000

For grammatical reasons, I wouldn't go along with *login to,* except in contexts like "Use your *login to* access valuable information." But if I were you, I'd be tempted to switch from *log on* to *log in* in your phrase.

Midnight

See *12:00* (that is, *Twelve o'clock*).

Mortified

"A friend and I were having a pleasantly heated discussion about the appropriate use of the word *mortified.* I've used it, and noticed its frequent use, to express horror or shock, as in 'I was *mortified* when I saw the chairman wearing Speedos at the swimming pool.' An informal lunchtime poll seems to affirm this usage. However, several dictionaries define *mortified* as mainly denoting humiliation or embarrassment—for example, 'In my dream I was *mortified* to find myself naked at work.' Can you adjudicate?"

But of course. Usage manuals and the overwhelming majority of recent newspaper citations in online databases agree with your friend and your dictionaries: *mortification* does mean "humiliation" or "embarrassment." At least it does when it isn't being used in relation to asceticism and religious penance (as in *mortification of the flesh,* "self-denial" or "self-punishment") or in one of its specialized obsolete or historical senses, none of which means anything like "horror" or "shock."

I wonder, though, whether a person might sometimes experience secondhand mortification. Could it be that you were mortified on the chairman's behalf when you saw him so scantily clad? I imagine that when Thomas Jefferson ordered a copy of a French book titled *Sur la Création du Monde, Un Système d'Organisation Primitive* and a contretemps resulted, Jefferson felt ashamed on our country's behalf. He wrote to his book dealer, in 1814, "I am really *mortified* to be told that, in the *United States of America* [this latter emphasis is Jefferson's], a fact like this can become a subject of inquiry, and of criminal inquiry too, as an offence against religion; that a question about the sale of a book can be carried before the civil magistrate." If anyone can be said to have used *mortified* correctly in such a context, it's the man who drafted our Declaration of Independence and Virginia's statute for religious freedom.

Mr., Mrs., Ms., or nothing

"My question concerns the proper way to address two people with the same last name living at the same address. I work for a nonprofit organization, and we receive donations from people who send in a check with two names or simply put their first names on a form—for example, *Jane and John Doe*. In our thank-you letter to them is it proper to say 'Dear *Mr. and Ms. Doe*' or should it be 'Dear *Ms. Doe and Mr. Doe*'? We don't like to assume they are husband and wife; hence we do not use *Mrs.* unless they fill out the form specifically stating *Mrs.* Also, which would be proper for the address: *Jane and John Doe* or *Ms. Jane and Mr. John Doe*?"

Even in these quick-to-take-offense days, I can't imagine why two people who have a joint checking account and the same last name would be annoyed at you for supposing that they *share* their name. People who are prickly about how they are referred to tend to make that clear in advance. A woman might sign her letter *Jane Doe (Mrs. John Doe),* for instance—and it is considerate to pick up on hints like this. Absent any such hint, *Mr. and Ms. Doe* will be fine in the salutation, and *John and Jane Doe* will be fine in the address. When using courtesy titles, it's traditional to put the man's first, but you may well prefer to follow whatever order the specific donors use.

Nude, Nuder, Nudest

"In the sense of 'unclothed,' *Merriam-Webster's Collegiate* shows *nuder* as an adjective: *nude, nuder, nudest.* How can one person be nuder than another? Either you are so or you are not. Will you please clarify?"

The *OED* doesn't specify in its entries for adjectives whether they may be "inflected" (made comparative and superlative using *-er* and *-est*), but surely there's a lesson in the fact that nowhere in the sixty million words of text of the *OED Online* does *nuder* or *nudest* appear. The *OED* does, after all, yield several instances apiece of the adjectives *wronger* and *wrongest,* even if some other reference books state or imply that these forms are, well, wrong.

Then again, a search of a recent year's worth of the publications catalogued in Nexis turned up three *nuder*s and three *nudest*s (not counting mentions of a Dr. Nuder, a mistaken reference to a "nudest resort," and so on) and five *more nude*s or *most nude*s. Here's an example, from *OC Weekly,* an Orange County, California, newspaper: "People are *nuder* in other places than they are here. I was walking in a park in Berlin once when I saw a man in his 60s sunning himself sublimely on the grass. Was he nude? Yes, he was!" And here's another, from *Harper's Bazaar,* in which the actress Sarah Jessica Parker is talking about a photo session for that magazine: "It was the *most nude* I have ever felt in my life." Evidently not everyone agrees that a person either is *nude* or is not.

That some people don't perceive nudity as an all-or-nothing proposition is further borne out by such frequently heard phrases as *totally nude* and *completely nude*—though those of us who are particular about our language tend to consider these phrases redundant and wrong. Nonetheless, *stark-naked* and *buck-naked* are perfectly acceptable folksy expressions, and they may be thought of as collateral evidence here.

My belief is that the failure to perceive *nude* as meaning something complete and logically uninflectable is one aspect of a widespread prejudice against small words: people don't always trust them to do their jobs. Besides *nuder* and *totally nude,* they say things like *ATM machine, armed gunman, free gift, visual image, mix together, future plans, general public,* and *very unique,* when *ATM, gunman, gift, image, mix, plans, public,* and *unique* would have worked just as hard for them— and done the job right.

Ñ *in proper names*

"As a person whose surname, Thomson, is consistently misspelled, I am perhaps unusually sensitive to this issue: major-league baseball persists in misspelling its players' Spanish surnames when they include the letter *ñ*. This baffles me. I e-mailed my local team, one of whose stars, Raul Ibañez, is an *ñ*-deprived player. I suggested that spelling his name with an *n* was equivalent to spelling Griffey *Griphey*. Since I received no response, I turn to you as the only institution with the power to compel major-league baseball to add *ñ* to its alphabet."

You and I know that you wrote and mailed your letter during an earlier baseball season. Ever since, I've been trying on your behalf to stir up some outrage among Hispanic ballplayers. Sorry, but I have had no success.

Though I didn't manage to talk with every major-league player whose name properly includes a tilde, as the diacritical mark in question is called, among those players with whom I was in touch—for instance, Fernando Viña, Roger Cedeño, and (through a spokesperson) Magglio Ordóñez—some do have tildes in their names as these appear on their uniforms, and generally they seemed pleased about that. But tildes rarely appear on scoreboards, and the players didn't seem particularly displeased about that. They recognize that scoreboards are harder to modify than uniforms. Lynn Lappin, the director of scoreboard operations for the Florida Marlins' stadium, in Miami, explained that if the stadium wanted to add tildes, "we'd have to change the keyboard mapping of the character generator"—quite a task. She added, "As it is, the character generator often crashes."

It is true that in Spanish the name Ibáñez, pronounced "Ee-*bon*-yes," would be considered misspelled if it didn't include a tilde, because Spanish treats *n* and *ñ* as separate letters of the alphabet, with distinct pronunciations (the Spanish *n* sounds like the *n* in "knuckleball," whereas *ñ* sounds like the *ny* in "nyuk-nyuk"). By insisting on tildes in English contexts, though, aren't we implicitly calling for characters like ň and ń, to use in other names?

Different purveyors of words will answer that question differently. *The Atlantic,* for instance, uses tildes but rarely the more exotic characters. The Associated Press never uses tildes or any other diacritical marks in its wire-service copy, because some AP newspapers' computers persist in misunderstanding them. If, as you say, in the world at large a name as simple as Thomson is routinely misspelled, then maybe a sports team that seeks out characters beyond the twenty-six letters of the English alphabet is just looking for trouble.

Ultimately, I think we need to shrug and tell ourselves that English is not a phonetic language, and that correctly pronouncing Raul Ibanez's name, so spelled, is really no trickier than pronouncing Gil Meche's. Furthermore, I have to admit that I'm relieved to have found anything related to ethnic identity about which the people in question are not poised to take offense but seem relaxed.

One of the only

"Where and how did the phrase *one of the only* start turning up? For example, recently I read 'Turkey is *one of the only* Muslim states to have had a female prime minister' in *The Christian Science Monitor,* which should know better. I see the phrase everywhere. Am I one of the only people to have noticed this?"

No, you're not. Those who like to ponder language may enjoy wondering why *the only ones* is good form while *one of the only* is not. Oh, well. *One of the only* isn't good form. Depending on meaning, choose *the only* or *one of the few* instead.

That exchange was published in Word Court, and you'll notice I breezed through my answer without citing any sources. Shortly after it was published, my colleague Linda Lowenthal sent me this e-mail:

"Personally, I can't get worked up about *one of the only.* Doesn't it just seem more emphatic than *one of the few?* Or like a way of saying *just about the only* or *the only one as far as I know?* I agree there are contexts in which that sort of vagueness is unwanted and you should find out whether it really is the only one—but you don't always need to do that. I mean, I can live without *one of the only,* but it doesn't bother me either."

I e-mailed her back:

Believe it or not, two *Atlantic* readers, within seven minutes of each other yesterday, sent me indignant e-mails protesting that they, too, had written to Word Court about the egregious *one of the only* and how dare I use someone else's letter in the column. One of them had even resurrected his original e-mail from . . . I think it was 1996. I've soothed them, but, boy, were they het up!

Truth to tell, none of the reference sources I rely on discusses this particular point. Under *one*, they tend to focus on explaining why or whether a sentence like the following, with a plural verb in the *that* clause and a singular main verb, is correct: "One of the books that *overlook* this point *is Garner's Modern American Usage.*" (Since you asked, I think that's correct—but so is "One of the topics that *Your Own Words addresses is* this," with two singular verbs. How can sentences on both patterns be right? Try recasting the two, in your own mind, in each case starting with the *of:* "Of the books that *overlook* this point, one *is Garner's* . . ." And "Of the topics that *Your Own Words addresses,* one *is* this.")

Under *only,* my references tend to be staking out their positions in the endless debate over whether that word must properly be placed next to the word it modifies ("I began to think about this *only* recently") or may be elsewhere in the sentence ("I *only* began to think about this recently"). (Since you asked, I always consider whether *only* might advantageously be moved, but I'm not strict about keeping it next to the word it modifies if that results in something awkward.)

But *one of the only* isn't covered. Now, I figure, the *AHD* defines the adjective *only* like this: "alone in kind or class; sole" and "standing alone by reason of superiority or excellence." And who in the world would be in favor of a construction like "*one of the lone* Muslim states" or "*one of the sole* Muslim states"? Note, too, what happens if we experiment with turning my correspondent's sentence around so that it starts with the *of.* No one—I hope— would say '*Of the only* Muslim states to have had a female prime minister, Turkey is one.' Surely we'd say "*Of the few* . . . " So there we have it.

I'm not completely alone in my opinion. Some grammar Web sites (and no doubt some books) make the case against *one of the only,* and, as you've seen, some *Atlantic* readers feel strongly about it. Still, here I've come almost as close to inventing a rule as you'll see me do.

Online, On line

"I write internal communication pieces for the employees of our energy, information, and technology company. I frequently encounter a style issue for which I cannot find an answer: When our company builds a new power-generating plant, we say it will come *on line* by a certain date. When someone refers to electronic communication, it is said to be *online.* Are these uses correct, or is *online* becoming the commonly used style for both applications? Help. We're dealing with this weekly."

The strongest support I can find for treating a power-generating plant the same as a computer appears in *The New York Times Manual.* Its entry for *online* reads: "Make it a solid compound in all references to electronic connections. By extension, the spelling also applies to places like factories (*The plant went online in August*), but that use is usually jargon."

Most current dictionaries, however, consider *online* or *on-line* in computer contexts to be distinct from *on line* in the sense of "coming into or being in operation." In this latter sense the term usually appears in the dictionary's *line* entry, as a two-word idiomatic expression. I think the forms as you have them in your letter are fine.

Pant, Pants

"One clothing store after another considers a pair of pants to be a *pant*. I say that's incorrect, but who am I? The stores are the ones who specialize in selling trousers. Then again, could they be wrong?"

A citation in the *OED* shows that much the same observation as you make about clothing stores was made about "clerks in dry-goods stores" by one H. A. Shands, who added, "Of course, *pants* is a well-known abbreviation [of *pantaloons*], but I think *pant* is rather a new word." These comments appeared in Shands's book *Some Peculiarities of Speech in Mississippi*, published in 1893. Today's dictionaries don't call *pant* wrong, but it seems to remain true that most people who use that form of the word are in the clothing trade.

The rest of us usually say *pants*—or *slacks, chinos, clam diggers, flares, jeans,* or what have you. But note that the word for any version of this item of clothing is plural; to refer specifically to any one such item, we must say *a pair of* . . . If people who talk about pants day in and day out sooner or later say "Let me show you a different *pant*," I can sympathize, though I don't plan to join them.

Point, Pointe

"The current tendency—in the South, anyway—to tack an *e* on *point*, as in *Plantation Pointe*, seems as ridiculous to me as *Ye Olde Shoppe* signs."

I like *pointe* still less than *Ye Olde Shoppe*, because at least there's a satisfying explanation for the latter. The *Y* in *Ye* originated in an Old English rune called thorn, which signified the sound *th* although it came to look like a capital *Y*; thorn persisted into Middle English times. Even then, however, there were no dictionaries to speak of, so people who wanted to spell had to improvise—hence the extra letters in *olde* and *shoppe.*

Obviously, none of this applies to the contemporary penchant for adding *e* to the ends of words—which is not exclusively a southern tendency, nor does it afflict only *point.* I fear that restaurants with the word *grille* in their names—a word that is supposed to describe ornamental metalwork and the like, as opposed to *grill,* which properly refers either to a device upon which food is cooked over an open flame or to a restaurant that features food so cooked—are spreading across our land like wildfire. I called the headquarters of the Capital Grille chain, hoping to learn what its founders had in mind when they named their first restaurant, in Providence, Rhode Island, in 1990. The good sport who got stuck answering the question used the word "elegant" twice and also explained that the *e* was meant to be "a nod toward tradition." That must be Ye olde tradition that fell out of fashion in the seventeenth century, when dictionaries came in.

More to the point is *pointe* itself. Some few *pointes* are distinctly French in origin—Grosse Pointe, Michigan, for example, and the ballet term *en pointe,* meaning "on tiptoe"—and these are hard to fault. But then there are places like your Plantation Pointe, a new development in South Carolina, and three Pointe or Pointe Hilton resorts, in greater Phoenix. The first of these resorts opened in 1976, under the name The Pointe at Squaw Peak, so it was probably on the leading edge of the trend you mention. A representative of the Pointe South Mountain Resort cheerfully reported that the *e* was used "I suppose to fancy it up." In recent years a public school, Mountain Pointe High School, was built near this latter resort. To come up with the school's name, "we just copied," a spokesperson for the school said. Oh, good.

Possessives of initialisms and acronyms

"What is the appropriate way to write the possessive of an organization's name while also introducing the acronym? For example, 'the National Science Foundation's (*NSF's*) most prestigious awards.'"

Write around this so that you don't have to put a possessive ending on the abbreviation: "the most prestigious awards given by the National Science Foundation (NSF)" or "the National Science Foundation (NSF) awards that are most prestigious." (Strictly speaking, your example is not an acronym but an initialism. When said aloud, initialisms, such as *NSF* and *NRA,* are spelled out letter by letter ["en-es-ef"], whereas acronyms, such as *NASA* and *NATO,* are pronounced as words ["nay-toe"].)

Although it's common practice to introduce an acronym or initialism parenthetically the first time the name of the organization comes up and then use the short version in subsequent mentions, writers sometimes get carried away. Before you know it, you're plowing blearily through sentences like "A PIN or other ID number is now required to access the NSF, NIH, and UNHCR databases, except on CD-ROM."

Unless you follow a stylebook that firmly decrees when and where acronyms and initialisms belong, you'll do well to ask yourself whether in any given case they are serving the reader or just introducing clutter. If the reference to the National Science Foundation appears in a report or an article that mentions the organization only once or twice more, it might be better to leave out the initialism and subsequently refer to "the foundation" or even repeat its full name.

Problematic

"Didn't the word *problematic* used to mean 'uncertain'—as in 'Whether Billy will come home for Thanksgiving is highly *problematic*'? My dictionary does give the sense 'attended by problems.' But saying that problems in a policy or a poem make it *problematic* would once have thudded on the ear. Bastard child of an ancient noun and a promiscuous suffix, *problematic* has now begotten, especially in academia, its own creepy spawn: *problematics, problematical, problematize,* even *problematicize.* What say you? Are *problematics* different from *obscurities* or *difficulties*?"

When a word is given new, more impressive duties, people can be so resentful! But if those duties are worth doing and the word can still handle its old job, too, what's the problem? Actually, the *OED* tells me, for some centuries *problematical* meant "troubling" or "troublesome" as well as "uncertain," while *problematic* (which can be traced back to 1609) tended to be restricted to that last meaning. Now *problematic* is more common in all senses—so what's happened is that the shorter form has taken over most of the longer one's work.

I'm more in sympathy with you about the noun *problematics* and those unwieldy verbs *problematize* and *problematicize.* Prob-

lematics began as sociological jargon, although, as you obviously know, it has gone interdisciplinary. *The Problematics of Moral and Legal Theory,* by Richard A. Posner; *Negotiating Unruly Problematics,* by Gearóid Ó Tuathail, Susan Roberts, and Andrew Herod— these are fairly typical uses in titles. Yes, these authors do mean something special by *problematics*—and if you want to know what they have in mind, you should read their work. But if you'll be satisfied by a quick and snarky definition of *problematize,* here is one that was offered by the writer Elizabeth Manus in *Salon* a few years ago: "In academia, reading a text in a new way is generally known as '*problematizing*' a text." Manus gave that explanation while reporting on a theory then being advanced by Carlyle V. Thompson, a literature professor, that F. Scott Fitzgerald's character Jay Gatsby was a black man passing for white.

Purpose, Purposes

"Is it correct to say 'The *purpose* of this report *is*' and then list two or more items, such as 'to define test methods and to clarify their applications'? I'm tripping over using 'The *purposes* of this report *are.*' The word *purposes* seems to inhabit the rhetorical domain or to turn up in set phrases like 'for all intents and *purposes.*' It's never followed by a list of anything! When I test it out and say 'The *purposes* of this book *are* to X, Y, and Z,' it sounds funny to me.

"I've looked everywhere for a source that spells out the use of this word, so that it can be correct in the engineering publications I edit. Can you help?"

Purpose is definitely singular, but I see what you mean about the illogic of telling people that a report has one purpose and then declaring that purpose to be a whole range of things. If the list to follow amounts to one complicated thing (for example, ". . . is to examine the evidence and present our conclusions"), I think *purpose* is just fine. If the list really does cover a bunch of things, though, why not change *purpose* to *goals* or revise the sentence to read "This report is intended to serve four *purposes*" or something like that?

Save . . . off, Save . . . on

"Which is correct? 'Save 20% *off* suggested retail price' or 'Save 20% *on* suggested retail price'?"

Does it have to be one or the other? "Save 20% *on* this product" seems fine to me. And "20% *off* the suggested retail price," without the *save,* seems fine as well. But there's something a bit odd about both versions you propose. *Save,* of course, is a word that in theory it's impossible to repeat too often in selling copy. To use it and preserve your meaning, how about "Save! Now 20% off the suggested retail price"?

Sex abuse, Sexual abuse

"What's with the phrase *sex abuse*? Lately I've been seeing and hearing it everywhere in relation to certain scandals. Wouldn't the correct phrase be *sexual abuse*?"

The term *sexual abuse* seems more literate to me, too, than *sex abuse.* When I began looking into your question, I expected to find that *sex abuse* was newly coined for, or at least newly common in, reports about recent scandals in the Roman Catholic

Church. But although the term *sex abuse* has never been as prevalent as the term *sexual abuse,* I was able to trace it back almost thirty years in Nexis citations—about as far back as Nexis citations go. Most dictionaries don't give either term, no doubt because both terms can be understood from their component parts. The only one of my current dictionaries with an entry for *sex abuse* is the *Random House Webster's Unabridged,* which cross-references it to *sexual abuse,* thus treating *sex abuse* as a variant.

Does this mean that you should avoid using the term *sex abuse*? In practice I think I might make the same decisions that *The New York Times Book Review* did in a recent issue. Narrow-measure text on the section's cover included the phrase *sex abuse* where *sexual abuse* would probably not have fit. Inside the section the review used *sexual abuse* consistently.

Single most, Single worst

"Could you please wave your magic wand and make the popular redundant hypersuperlative disappear forever? I've had it up to here with 'the *single most important* scientific discovery of the century' and 'the *single worst* disaster in aviation history.'"

I agree with you that *single* in phrases like your examples adds clutter instead of the emphasis that is surely intended. Unfortunately, nothing short of sorcery is likely to get rid of it. *Single most, single worst,* and so forth are very common, and I can find only a single, mild objection to them in any of the major usage guides: *The New Fowler's Modern English Usage* mentions that *single most* is "in strict terms . . . tautologous."

Skies, Sky

"I have been in and around the broadcasting business for most of my life, and one aspect of weather forecasting has always made me mad. When referring to that which is above us, the forecasters generally speak of *skies.* You will have to help me, because I cannot find the end of one sky and the start of another. Wouldn't it be 'expect a partly cloudy *sky* tomorrow'?"

"Oh, give me a home where the buffalo roam, where the deer and the antelope play; where seldom is heard a discouraging word, and the *sky* is not cloudy all day." "Blue days, all of them gone; nothing but blue *sky* from now on." "O beautiful for a spacious *sky,* for amber waves of grain . . ." Nah. Forget about it. Just forget about it. *Skies* is a perfectly good word.

Snarky

"I just read a column of yours [see *Problematic,* earlier in this chapter] in which you gave what you called 'a quick and snarky definition' of a certain word. But how were you using *snarky*? The *OED Supplement* gives 'irritable' as a definition. The Web site www.urbandictionary.com gives 'a combination of sarcasm and cynicism. Usually accepted as a complimentary term.' From context, I thought you might mean something akin to *quick and dirty,* as that phrase is used to refer to a repair that's not done by the book, a shortcut, or an improvisation."

It's true that most print dictionaries, including the *OED,* don't define *snarky* as it's now being used—though that Web site of yours, a dictionary of slang whose users update it continually, has it right. (*Snarky* does appear in *Merriam-Webster's Collegiate* with much the same meaning.) But when I looked at Nexis recently, it showed me sixty-six citations from American newspapers and newswires in the previous week alone. At a glance it seemed that none of them intended the word to mean, simply, "irritable," and virtually all of them used it the way I meant to. Though I felt a twinge of guilt about using an unusual word whose current meaning readers can't find in most dictionaries, *snarky* struck me as a word whose time has come and as the perfect word for that context.

Sweet tooths

"A recent wire-service article about Marshmallow Peeps included a line about the manufacturer celebrating its fiftieth year of 'satisfying *sweet tooths*.' Is *sweet tooths* correct?"

Yes. If I were ordered at gunpoint to justify *sweet teeth* instead, I could do it easily enough: the singular is *sweet tooth*, the plural of *tooth* is *teeth*, so the plural of *sweet tooth* must be *sweet teeth*. But *The New Oxford American Dictionary* gives *sweet tooths* as the plural of *sweet tooth*. (Our other dictionaries are no more forthcoming than they were back in Chapter Two when we wanted to know the plural of *wildlife*.) The thing to focus on is that the *tooth* in *sweet tooth* isn't really a *tooth*, singular, in the literal sense of a molar, a bicuspid, or an incisor, so *sweet tooth* needn't follow the rules that would apply to literal *tooth* compounds, like *front tooth, front teeth.* Consider *sabertooth* and *sabertooths*. (Dictionaries will tend to tell you that these are properly referred to as *saber-toothed cats* or *saber-toothed tigers,* and these are the usual forms in edited media as well, but *sabertooth* is about twice as common as *saber-toothed* on Web sites in general, while *saberteeth* is extremely rare.) And in the online game EverQuest, Kerra Ridge is where *sharptooths*—not *sharpteeth*—live.

It's more often linguists than prescriptive grammarians who explain things like this about plurals. But from linguists' point of view, what is "correct" is simply that which most English-speakers would come up with when asked. That *is* the basis of our language, so if the prescriptive grammarians haven't weighed in on a particular question, they can scarcely complain if we poll edited media to try to find a consensus. When I checked Google News for the past month's worth of citations, it showed me six *sweet tooths* and two *sweet teeth.* When I checked Nexis for the past month's worth from U.S. newspapers and newswires, it showed me fifteen *sweet tooths* and four *sweet teeth.* So, as I said, the latter form can be justified, or at least some professional editors *are* justifying it and using it. But the former form is more common and, to my mind, preferable.

Terror, Terrorist

"How and when did the word *terror* begin to replace *terrorist* as an adjective (as in *terror attacks*)? *Terror* is also being used interchangeably with *terrorism,* as in *the war on terror.*"

The adjectival use of *terror* has been with us for some time. Searching the Nexis database for U.S. news stories published on a recent spring day and also on the same day of the year in 2000 and 2001, before September 11, I found citations in reputable papers in each year for the likes of *terror attack* and *terror organization,* as well as *terrorist attack* and *terrorist organization.* The *terrorist* versions were and remain considerably more common, though.

Neither *war on terrorism* nor *war on terror* was a common phrase in earlier years; now, alas, neither is rare. But *war on terrorism* does appear a good deal more often than *war on terror.* If I were you, I'd prefer the forms *terrorist* and *terrorism* to *terror,* but I'd accept *terror* without protest when others use it.

Three times a year

"I'm contacting you with this question out of sheer desperation. There's nowhere else to turn. Is there a word that means 'happening three times a year'?"

Some dictionaries give *triannual* with this meaning. Unfortunately, *triannual* can also mean "happening once every three years." That is, it is sometimes also considered a synonym of *triennial.* As with *biannual* and *biennial,* the former having two meanings and the latter always meaning "happening every two years," we might wish there were a logical and tidy distinction between the words, but there isn't, and pretending otherwise is only going to get everybody confused. Why not just say *three times a year?* Though it takes up more space in writing, it has no more syllables than *triannual.*

Too

"I have what seems to be a minor grammatical question, yet I cannot find an answer in any book. I wonder if you can tell me why one often finds a comma before *too* in a sentence like this: 'She likes ice cream, *too.*' I would appreciate any answer, insight, or historical explanation you have."

I can tell you what *The Atlantic*'s rule is about commas with *too,* and I will also tell you that my colleague Martha Spaulding and I made it up, because we couldn't find an established rule that we liked. When *too* is next to the word it modifies, put commas around it, because in speech, noticeable pauses are likely to occur. When *too* appears elsewhere in the sentence, don't use commas, because speakers are less likely to pause. Thus: "At least one other person, *too,* has written me about this punctuation question. I used to wonder about it *too.*" This rule works pretty well in about nine out of ten cases.

By *The Atlantic*'s lights, then, your example, "She likes ice cream, *too,*" would be correctly punctuated if she also likes— oh, say, cookies or cigarettes or pouring sugar in her mouth straight out of little packets. But if the idea is that she as well as her husband likes ice cream, you'd delete the comma or make it "She, *too,* likes ice cream."

Traditional

"What on earth has befallen the poor word *traditional*? It is now so widely used to mean 'typical; usual; common' that it seems in danger of losing its, well, traditional meaning. This morning I read in the paper that the use of prescription drugs is growing faster among children than it is among 'senior citizens and baby boomers, the two *traditionally* high consumer groups.' What is that tradition? Is it like Nativity scenes at Christmas, the Easter bunny, the display of the flag on the Fourth of July? Recently I have encountered the notions that *traditionally* males outnumber females in certain occupations, that *traditionally* high school dropout rates are higher among Hispanic students, that *traditionally* the stock market goes down under certain circumstances, and on and on. Is there nothing that can be done?"

The adverb *traditionally,* more than the adjective *traditional,* does indeed often stray from the usual meaning of *tradition:* a custom or practice intentionally handed down through the generations. That is, *traditionally* is often pressed into service to characterize things that were, simply, typical or common in the past. Drift like this isn't particularly unusual in English, though. *Particular,* for instance, has at least one familiar sense, "choosy," that isn't reflected in *particularly,* and the idea of an exception doesn't necessarily come to mind when one reads *exceptionally,* which for the most part is a fancy substitute for *very.* In any case, I think there *is* nothing that can, or should, be done to drag *traditionally* back to its roots.

Triannual, Triennial

See *Three times a year.*

Turned up missing

See *Gone missing.*

Turn of the century

"In producing a book on American art circa 1900, we find ourselves in a quandary. Does the phrase *turn of the century* refer to the century that is ending or the one that is beginning? Is circa

1900 *the turn of the nineteenth century* or *the turn of the twentieth*? Please advise."

My understanding is that the phrase is like *turn of the tide*, in that it refers to the switchover, the process by which one thing becomes something else, rather than to one or the other tide, or century. Dictionaries tend to support this view. For example, the *AHD* has among its definitions for the noun *turn*, "A point marking the end of one period of time and the beginning of the next: *the turn of the century.*" And the *OED* has: "The point at which one named period of time gives way to the next; the beginning or end *of* a named period of time, regarded in relation to the transition point between it and the preceding or following period; *specifically (a) turn of the century*, the beginning or end of the century under consideration."

So I'd suggest that you establish a context of about a hundred years ago and then just use the phrase *the turn of the century*, rather than specifying *the turn of the nineteenth century* or . . . *of the twentieth century*. Alternatively, you could recast the sentence to say *as the nineteenth century drew to a close* or *at the outset of the twentieth century* or the like.

I should add that this is what *I* think. When I conducted a Nexis search for *turn of the twentieth century*, I found numerous citations for the phrase from newspapers and magazines, including some of the best. And *Webster's Third* includes the citation "years *at the turn of the twentieth century* were vintage years." A hunt through about a dozen style and usage manuals turned up no advice about how to use *turn of the. . .* , except in my own *Word Court: Wherein Verbal Virtue Is Rewarded, Crimes Against the Language Are Punished, and Poetic Justice Is Done* (2000).

12:00

"The organization I work for published the following sentence: 'The new five-channel 60-meter allocation becomes available to US Amateur Radio operators at *midnight (12:00 A.M.)* local time on July 3.' The Federal Communications Commission established the effective time.

"Two readers—one of them arguing quite vehemently—said this was misleading. I concede that *midnight* can mean different things to different people, but there ought to have been no confusion once we defined *midnight* in terms of the precise time involved: 12:00 A.M. The more vehement reader disagreed, suggesting that the term *midnight* just muddied the waters and we should have just said 'at *12:00 A.M.* local time.' He contended that *midnight on July 3* 'does NOT, I repeat, does NOT mean the start of the day July 3' (emphasis his). Just ask anybody, he challenged. My response to him was that a lot of people believe midnight to be 12:00 *P.M.,* not 12:00 A.M., so more than a few may have thought we meant midday, not midnight, when the new day starts. Therefore, I asserted, both expressions were necessary. My editors had no problem with my wording, nor did a majority of readers, apparently; they showed up on the air at the appointed hour. What's your take on this? My feeling is the next time we run into this one, we'll just arbitrarily make it read *12:01 A.M.,* omit any mention of *midnight,* and let the chips fall."

On the one hand, *M.* is an abbreviation of *meridies,* which means "noon" in Latin. *A.M.* and *P.M.* are short for *ante meridiem* and *post meridiem,* which mean "before noon" and "after noon." So I suppose in theory both *12:00 A.M.* and *12:00 P.M.* could be thought of as midnight—but it isn't generally considered good form to use either term. *Midnight* will do it.

On the other hand, though, *is* "midnight on July 3" the beginning or the end of the day? According to both the *Associated Press Stylebook* and *The New York Times Manual,* midnight ends the day. I think you're right to write around the problem from now on: ". . . at the outset in local time (12:00:01) of July 3," or something like that.

After that exchange was published, I received this follow-up letter:

"The solution you offered in your final sentence seemed awkward to me. The problem was that I couldn't think of anything better. Nor could my writing colleague, whom I consulted after reading the column. The next day I happened to mention the dilemma to my husband, an accountant. He suggested something to the effect of 'The new channel allocation becomes available after midnight, on the morning of July 3.' This solution seemed as clear and simple as any we had come up with. Leave it to an accountant to show up a bunch of copywriters!"

Valuable, Invaluable

See *Flammable, Inflammable.*

Was, Were

See *If.*

Weedate

"I am wondering about the past tense of *weedeat*—as in 'used a weedeater.' Do I say 'I weedate the back forty'? One of my friends avoids the problem by calling the device a *weedwhacker,* thus enabling the past tense to be *weedwhacked.*"

Boy, are you in trouble—not with me but with Frigidaire Home Products, which owns the Weed Eater brand, and also with Sears Craftsman, which owns Weedwacker. These companies are anxious lest their brand names go the way of *aspirin* and *escalator*—erstwhile trademarks that became generic through their owners' failure to defend them vigorously.

Seriously, though, each of us must decide to what extent to defer to corporate sensibilities in our language. Should we try to avoid using *Xerox* as a verb or as a name for the output of a Canon photocopier? Is it OK to offer a guest a *Kleenex* when Puffs is the only brand of facial tissues in the house? Dare we even speak of *weed-eating* or *weed-whacking*?

In all these cases trademarks are being encroached on. It may be that few care except representatives of the relevant corporations and the nation's copy editors. Copy editors, though, are exactly who prevent generic uses of trademarks from becoming standard, by keeping them out of printed sources. And they do keep them out often enough that in good-quality edited English, generic uses of brand names are the exception, not the rule.

If you're just talking with your friends and neighbors, certainly feel free to say anything you like: *weed-ate, weed-eated, Weed Eatered,* whatever. If, though, you find yourself wanting to work a reference to operating your Weed Eater™ or your friend's Weedwacker™ into something like a speech or a letter to the editor of your newspaper, you'll seem better attuned to the complexities of modern life if you follow the advice of the spokesman for Frigidaire whom I consulted. He recommends that you say *trimmed.*

Who, Whom

"I'd love your help with the following: '. . . and to ensure they know *who* to call in an emergency.' Shouldn't it be '*whom* to call'? I recently came across this construction in a manuscript that I was editing and confidently changed *who* to *whom.* But since doing so, I've begun to doubt my choice. Is this phrase somehow an exception to the rule? Why does it sound awkward: because it's incorrect or simply because we are by now so accustomed to hearing *who* when *whom* is correct? I've consulted numerous grammar guides and discussed it with a co-worker, and all roads seem to lead back to *whom.* But then, just as I was beginning to feel reassured about my original edit, I heard an NPR announcer say ' . . . *who* to consult,' and this threw me right back into the quagmire of doubt and second-guessing."

You're right that correct grammar does require "*whom* to call." You'd say "They know to call *him* [objective case] in an emergency"—and so also correct are "They know to call *whom* [objective]" and "They know *whom* to call."

Nonetheless, more than a few authorities on language look askance at *whom* even where it's grammatically correct. William Safire once wrote, "The best rule for dealing with *who* vs. *whom* is this: Whenever *whom* is required, recast the sentence." And here's Calvin Trillin on the same subject: "As far as I'm concerned, 'whom' is a word that was invented to make everyone sound like a butler." So you would be in good company if you preferred to do some tinkering with your sentence. How about ". . . and to ensure they know the right person to call"?

Would

See *If.*

CHAPTER NINE

Your Own Words

Does being able to answer questions about language with confidence allow a person to communicate fluently? Well, it's a start. We have been focusing on the materials of language—individual words and phrases—as opposed to the processes of writing and speaking. Language at this broader level is the focus of writing guides and guides to communication. (*Communication* is an unlovely word, but it does include speech. And it's more to the point than *expressing yourself*, because *communication* suggests interaction, being in touch with others, taking care to be understood.) These guides aren't reference works, like the resources we've discussed to this point. As we've seen, even standard references are much more subjective than many people think. But guides to communication are more subjective still: their authors are telling you what has worked for them. Let's look at four of them while bearing in mind that what we really want to know is what will work for you.

Untold numbers of books, articles, classes, workshops, and Web sites are devoted to how to speak and write well. Some of these are highly specific, detailing how to become a storyteller, how to write technical manuals, how to coin new words that will have staying power, how to negotiate conversations about difficult subjects, how to tell jokes. The books we'll review, though, consider a wide range of verbal expression and are time-tested, with large and grateful followings.

Probably the best known of all American writing guides is *The Elements of Style,* by William Strunk Jr. and E. B. White. Its first edition, by Strunk alone, was a "forty-three-page summation of the case for cleanliness, accuracy, and brevity in the use of English," as White wrote in his introduction to later editions. Strunk, who taught English at Cornell, published the book privately in 1918 and began assigning it to his students, one of whom the next year was E. B. White. White, of course, went on to become the author of countless lovely, pithy essays that appeared in *The New Yorker* over a half century beginning in 1925, and also of twenty-some books, including the children's classics *Charlotte's Web* and *Stuart Little.* Almost forty years after his course with Strunk, who had in the meantime died, White was commissioned to revise and expand *The Elements of Style;* he added a new chapter, "An Approach to Style." Now the book is in its fourth edition (1999) and weighs in at 123 pages, including a foreword by White's stepson, Roger Angell.

The Elements of Style is justly famous. And yet if we study it in the same unblinking way we've studied our reference works, we'll see that virtually every "rule" and "principle" in it has generally acknowledged exceptions, some of which are explained in the book and some of which are not; or the rule or principle is a choice, an expression of taste, and many good writers habitually choose otherwise; or it sums up something complicated that is hard to apply unless you know a good deal more than is explained in *The Elements of Style* itself.

For instance, Part I, "Elementary Rules of Usage," opens with "*1. Form the possessive singular of nouns by adding* 's." Connoisseurs of books' first sentences will not be impressed. And is that really the first thing anyone needs to know about writing? The discussion that follows gives exceptions—not idiosyncratic ones, to be sure, but also not quite the same exceptions as appear in the *Associated Press Stylebook* (which is, you'll remember, one of the country's most widely followed stylebooks), *The New York Times Manual of Style and Usage,* or a number of other standard reference works.

The second rule given is *"In a series of three or more terms with a single conjunction, use a comma after each term except the last."* That is, Strunk and White are calling for serial commas—a rule that reference works again including the *AP Stylebook* and *The New York Times Manual* flatly tell their readers not to follow.

Third comes *"Enclose parenthetic expressions between commas,"* and the ensuing discussion will familiarize beginners with this sound idea. But Strunk and White don't present a complete set of guidelines for deciding what is and what is not a parenthetic expression. Nobody could and still have room to say much else in a 123-page book. If we convened a panel of authorities on language, I promise you we could get a vigorous argument going about, for instance, whether the date in this sentence is parenthetic: "By the time Elvis Presley died, in 1977, the mainstream of popular music had moved on: Rod Stewart had the No. 1 song that year, and Presley's best showing on the pop chart was No. 64." (A person can't die more than once, so the year in which Presley died is an extra fillip of information, not something we need in order to understand what is meant by his death—so from this point of view, the date is parenthetic. But by when had the mainstream moved on; what year was it when Rod Stewart had the No. 1 song? Far from being parenthetic, some will say, the date is essential to understanding the main point of the sentence.)

I am fond of *The Elements of Style* and am dissecting it so ruthlessly only because it has a reputation for teaching universal truths about writing. But that is not what it does. At best, it teaches people how to write like E. B. White. This is no mean accomplishment—though as I said, that's at best. At worst, the book's advice is turned into clichés and misinterpreted. For instance, a widely repeated dictum from Part II, "Elementary Principles of Composition," is *"Omit needless words."* Exactly what words, where, are needless, please?

The letter that follows came in to Word Court just the other day. Its author doesn't quote Strunk and White, but their influence on him, direct or indirect, is clear.

"One of the persistent irritations of reading or listening is the overuse of the word *back,* even by notable writers and speakers. It is as though they're paid by the word.

"For example, *back in 1974.* The year 1974 is already *back;* 1974 is not future or present—it is past. *Back in* is totally redundant and adds nothing to a past tense. Even a careless writer would avoid the redundancies of this sentence: '*Back in 1948* a poor destitute widow woman met a rich millionaire, and *back in 1949* they celebrated their marriage nuptials.'

"Yours for less careless writing and speaking."

Sigh.

Yes, but there's the matter of tone. Consider "*Way back in 1974,* when Barbra Streisand had the year's No. 1 song . . ." The phrase is meant to take us, um, back—to evoke nostalgia—and plain old *in 1974* doesn't do the job nearly as well. In something like a history of the Vietnam War, the brisk factuality of *in 1974* might be preferable; few of us consider Vietnam anything to wax nostalgic about. But Streisand's "The Way We Were," her No. 1 song that year, was nostalgic even when it was new; even then it was summoning listeners *back*. Some words evoke feeling, convey nuance, rather than just supplying information. You're right to ask whether a given instance of *back* serves a purpose; many don't. But others do, and just because the purpose is subtle, that doesn't mean we should overlook it.

I am not alone in feeling that what words are needless is highly subjective. Here's what Bill Walsh has to say in *The Elephants of Style:*

I'm closer to the "Punch it up a bit" school of writing than I am to "Just the facts, ma'am." I attach a big asterisk to the "Omit needless words" credo from the original "Elements," and I roll my eyes at "Simple, declarative sentences," another mantra that many chant but few follow. I think writing, in most cases, should be writing, not just an owner's-manual-style recitation of what you need to know. I like a little writing with my writing.

I doubt that even Strunk and White, if we had them here with us, would disagree. Their discussion of *"Omit needless words"* explains, "This requires not that the writer make all sentences short, or avoid all detail and treat subjects only in outline, but that every word tell." Though I like that explanation, I'm not sure how much further it will take a resistant mind than *"Omit needless words."* Would the man who is irritated by *back* agree with me that *back* at least sometimes tells?

Another point I want to make here is implicit in the title of White's best-known book of essays, *One Man's Meat*. That title is, ultimately, derived from an aphorism that Lucretius coined in the first century B.C.: "What is food to one man may be fierce poison to others."

Indeed, according to what I've heard over the years from avid fans of Joseph M. Williams's *Style: Toward Clarity and Grace*, many of them have been humiliated, or at least underwhelmed, by *The Elements of Style*. It just never worked for them, and what Strunk and White fans consider wise, these people consider maddeningly vague. Williams eggs them on, actively cultivating his market niche as the anti–Strunk and White. *Style* (which was first published in 1981 and is now in its fourth edition, from 1990) begins: "This is a book about writing clearly. I wish it could be short and simple like some others more widely known, but I want to do more than just urge writers to 'Omit Needless Words' or 'Be clear.'"

Style is intended primarily for people who must write business or scholarly reports and articles, and members of this tribe will find in it many original, thought-provoking ideas to help improve their prose. The book is unstinting, with copious explanation and even diagrams and charts. I've worked with writers who I wish had read and taken to heart Williams's advice before they ever wrote a word for me. For my own part, though, my enthusiasm is guarded for a writing coach who, as Williams does, presents sentences like these as examples of good writing:

I do not know why my staff cannot find evidence to explain why we haven't been able to solve this problem in the ways we have before.

Our programs create varied "corporate" curricular personalities, particularly through their "introductory," "survey," or "foundational" courses.

Scientists have finally unraveled the mysteries of the human gene, a discovery that may lead to the control of such dread diseases as cancer and birth defects.

I'm not being quite fair here. Williams uses these examples to illustrate ways to improve writing that, I agree, is worse. But still. The three negatives in the first sentence make my head spin, and the idea of solving a current problem—"this problem"—"in the ways we have before" doesn't make sense. How about "in the ways we've solved earlier ones"? The very idea of the second sentence strikes me as creepy, and the quotation marks in it are hideous. And in the third sentence, "a discovery . . ." is what grammarians call an appositive, but an appositive is supposed to be in apposition to—connecting to and synonymous with or explaining—a noun. Let's look for a noun that means "discovery" in the main clause. Hmm. And "unraveled the mysteries" and "dread diseases" are pitiful clichés—and are birth defects a "disease"? Nonetheless, people who must write, particularly on technical subjects and even if they don't feel like it, may find much of value in this book. (If you suspect you are such a person, have a look at the glowing—and informative—reader reviews on Amazon.com.)

A third book that people swear by is William Zinsser's *On Writing Well* (published in 1976 and now in its sixth edition, from 2001). This one is for people who don't want a quality-control specialist to monitor their every pencil mark or keystroke but, rather, a wise mentor to urge them on. Large sections of *On Writing Well* are explicitly about what has worked for Zinsser: among the examples he uses to demonstrate his points are drafts of his own articles in various genres.

A cover line on the current edition of *On Writing Well* reads "More Than One Million Copies Sold"—and the book has earned its broad audience, for Zinsser offers unusual insights about the whole enterprise of writing. His chief concern is emotional substance. A "personal transaction" is "at the heart of good nonfiction writing," he argues. "Out of it come two of the most important qualities that this book will go in search of: humanity and warmth." He also says, "Ultimately the product that any writer has to sell is not the subject being written about, but who he or she is."

Though Zinsser no doubt means this to be encouraging, it is actually very bad news for dull or self-deluded people who want or have to write. Who and what a person is is almost impossible to conceal in writing—or speech. You know a corporate toady when you hear one, no? You know it when someone is speaking from the heart or is striving for an eloquence beyond his or her reach. When Zinsser says that our words will or won't "sell" who we are, I believe him. But this implies that if we want our words to be well received, we should begin by striving to be someone we can be proud of. Note, please: not that we should work on our self-esteem, but that we should work to *deserve* self-esteem.

It's strange that none of the books we're dipping into emphasizes that to communicate effectively a person needs to have something to say. All of them seem to take it for granted that everyone does have a message worth communicating. That's not my experience, though. People will go on and on describing the most ordinary things from the most ordinary points of view. Bless Zinsser for coming out in favor of human interest and the need to keep in mind that communicating is a "transaction"—a conversation. A writer is nothing without readers.

Is it clear that these three writing guides are no more alike than the dictionaries we studied in earlier chapters? And yet each of them sits squarely within the literary, journalistic, and scholarly traditions I've inhabited my whole life. There's very little they could possibly say that would strike me like a bolt from the blue. For that reason, I suppose, I find Dale Carnegie's *How to Win Friends and Influence People* (first published in 1936 and revised in 1981) to be more thought-provoking still. I know—Dale Carnegie? Of thirty principles in his book, however, all but one are about verbal communication. (The exception, in the section called "Six Ways to Make People Like You," is "Smile," and even that amounts to a metaphor about how to communicate with words.) According to the cover of the current paperback edition, *How to Win Friends* has sold more than fifteen million copies—so let's not be snobby.

Though *How to Win Friends* includes anecdotes about writers and quotes admiringly from letters and books, Carnegie has talk in mind much more than writing. And he clearly believes that if you meet the world with the right attitude, the words to express that attitude will come. In brief, his argument is that to get what we want (eventually), we should forget about what we want, try to figure out what the person we're talking to wants, and zero in on that. In fact, we already know some things the person we're talking to wants: our appreciation, our understanding, our help. All we have to do is offer those things—sincerely—and our interlocutor will be putty in our hands.

Carnegie ignores niceties of phrasing in favor of this point of view, and he doesn't devote so much as a sentence to parts of speech. Here's the kind of advice that Carnegie gives: "If out of reading this book you get just one thing—an increased tendency to think always in terms of other people's point of view, and see things from their angle—if you get that one thing out of this book, it may easily prove to be one of the building blocks of your career."

That, by the way, is a very badly written sentence. It has a bait-and-switch quality and seems to promise much more than it actually does. Shouldn't "If out of reading this book you get just one thing . . ." be followed by something like "that one thing ought to be . . . "? Shouldn't the thought end with a promise of something exuberant and life-changing? But the sentence wanders off into the wimpy "it may easily prove to be one of the building blocks of your career." All the same, it feels exuberant, like the rest of *How to Win Friends.* Carnegie does want, passionately, to change his readers' lives.

Carnegie's precepts, like Strunk and White's, have become clichés in certain circles—repeated out of context and misinterpreted. For instance, Carnegie is the guy to blame when salespeople tiresomely insert your first name into every sentence they say: Principle 3 among the "Six Ways to Make People Like You" is "Remember that a person's name is to that person the sweetest and most important sound in any language." But Carnegie's idea that a person's subject, the point of what someone is saying or writing, should be *you,* the recipient of it, is much like the idea that lies at the heart of the book you're now reading—the book you've almost finished reading, I mean.

The End

The truth is (and surely you know this by now), no single guide to communication can possibly meet *your* needs perfectly—any more than any dictionary or stylebook or usage manual will tell you everything you might want it to. In my experience, people are fearless about asking language questions. May this book help you be equally fearless in seeking answers. I have ceased to believe, as I once did, that there is no such thing as a silly question—about language or anything else. But sometimes even silly questions have intelligent, illuminating answers. By gathering information and thinking critically we can make these answers our own.

When all is said and done, we're each on our own with language. In this most collaborative of human endeavors, consensus at any level is rare. This paradox, rather than giving us license, though, challenges us to be exacting with ourselves even as we are judicious and broadminded with others. Amen.

INDEX